BELIEVE IT OR NOT

To Nick Greenwood for whom this book was originally written but who died of cancer before he could read it

Believe It or Not

A Sceptic's Guide To Christian Faith

JOHN H HEIDT

GRACEWING, LEOMINSTER

First Published in 1992
Gracewing
Fowler Wright Books
Southern Ave, Leominster
Herefordshire HR6 0QF

Gracewing Books are distributed

In New Zealand by
Catholic Supplies Ltd
80 Adelaide Rd
Wellington
New Zealand

In Australia by
Charles Paine Pty
8 Ferris Street
North Parramatta
NSW 2151 Australia

In Canada by
Novalis
PO Box 990
Outremont H2V 457
Canada

In USA by
Morehouse Publishing
P.O. Box 1321
Harrisburg
PA 17105
U.S.A.

All rights reserved. No part of this publication may be reproduced, stored in a retrieval system, or transmitted in any form, or by any means, electronic, mechanical, photocopying, recording, or otherwise, without the written permission of the publisher.

© *Text* John H Heidt 1992
© *Illustrations* Sean Morris 1992

Typesetting by SS Philip & James Church,
Up Hatherley, Cheltenham and
Action Typesetting, Gloucester

Printed and bound in Great Britain by
Billings and Son Ltd., Worcester

ISBN 0 85244 188 6

Contents

Foreword
By Way of Introduction

1	Introducing the Case of the Disappearing Atheists	3
2	A Plea for Scepticism	13
3	The Battle of the Gods	29
4	Public Revelations	45
5	Pain and Grief	61
6	All You Need Is Love	75
7	God in the Flesh	87
8	Jesus' Uprising	103
9	The Invisible Man	117
10	Beyond Belief	131
11	A New Beginning	143

Suggestions for Further Reading   155

Foreword

Many people may regret the fact, but undoubtedly it is a fact — that during the present century the Christian churches have sharply declined both in numbers and influence. Of course, the decline had begun more than two hundred years ago, at the time we call the Enlightenment, but it has accelerated and as yet no end appears to be in sight. The Christian heritage that maintained the spiritual life of the western nations throughout most of their history is increasingly marginalised.

No doubt many reasons could be given for this state of affairs, but I think that David Edwards was correct when he wrote a few years ago, "The basic problem confronting the churches is unbelief". The steady progress of the natural sciences and the amazing powers which they have brought has put a question mark against the need for faith, prayer and worship. I do not myself accept that Christianity has been discredited by the intellectual advances of modern times, and the evidence for this is that many men and women who are leaders in different fields of endeavour, including the sciences, find meaning and direction for their activities in Christian faith. But I do accept that there has to be more thinking in the churches. People will not believe just because their ancestors did. If they are thinking people, they ask quite reasonably that they should be shown the grounds for faith, just as they are shown the grounds for other beliefs they are asked to accept.

John Heidt has responded to the demand in this book. In the course of a varied ministry in both England and the United States, he has, so to speak, tuned in to the thinking of serious-minded men and women and has learned to communicate to them the essential truths of Christianity in terms that are current in the contemporary world.

Christianity is more than a set of beliefs to be received by the intellect. It is a whole way of life - in the current jargon, it is orthopraxis (right conduct) as well as orthodoxy (right belief). One of the strengths of this book is that it relates the Christian message firmly to the life of the practising Christian community. John Heidt is a theologian, but he is more - he is also a pastor who has brought vigourous new life to a sprawling urban parish, where the church is not a hold-out from the past but a wellspring of spiritual energy. It is in fact another living proof that the Christian faith, rightly and faithfully communicated, has lost none of its power to bring meaning and enhancement into human lives.

Pastors and people alike have much to learn from this book.

John Macquarrie

By Way of Introduction

Books no more than people ever have a single author. God may be my creator, but parents, friends and an almost infinite variety of social influences have gone to make me what I am. So it is with this book. Though I claim authorship it is the product of more people than I can possibly remember and of influences far greater than I can ever imagine.

Above all it is the product of the young people of my parish, of Vicki, Claire, Paul and Mark and all those others whose doubts forced me to recall how I came to my own beliefs when I was their age. In what follows I have tried to say what we never have an opportunity of saying in casual conversation, and if it does not convince them I hope it will at least help them understand why millions of people throughout the world think the way I do and why our thinking may just possibly make sense.

Given that this book belongs primarily to these young people I am especially pleased that one of them, Sean Morris, has agreed to do the illustrations. In some ways they are fanciful and even fantastic but that is all to the good in the world of Christian faith where human fantasy becomes fact and the incredible the only thing worth believing.

Though prefaces and introductions and even titles appear first in a book they are almost always written last, and this is no exception. My mind went down many winding and tortuous paths in an attempt to find an appropriate title and in the process I came up with several rather good ones and a few too embarrassing even to mention, but none seemed quite right until, talking about my dilemma in a London pub with my daughter and some of her friends, one of them, Glyn Giles, asked, 'Why not call it "Believe it or not"'? And so I have. Many years ago there was a series of cartoons syndicated in American newspapers called, 'Believe It or Not' by Ripley, in which he described different natural phenomena seemingly impossible to believe but in fact actually quite real. The same is true of Christian faith. We may believe it or not, but no amount of belief or scepticism will ever change the facts one way or the other, no matter how incredible these facts may appear.

It is one thing to know what you want to say and quite another to learn how to say it. Writing is never easy at the best of times and more difficult when it has to be done in the early hours of the morning before starting the work of a large and busy parish. The task would have never been completed if it had not been for my publishers who first saw that the original manuscript might eventually turn into a readable book. That you now have the present book in your hands is as much due to their patience and encouragement, and especially to that of Sheridan Swinson, as to anything else.

Awards for patience must also go to the assistant clergy of the parish who after Morning Prayer had to endure many descriptions of my latest attempts, and to my family for reassuring me when I was about ready to throw in the whole project. But above all an award for patience must go to Kathy Davies who proof-read so many versions of every chapter that by now she must know the entire book by heart.

Looking over the final product I realize that it is still far from perfect, but I must leave it as it is. What I have written no longer belongs to me anyway but to you. You will make of it what you will so that in the end there will be, as there have always been, as many books as there are readers and as many varieties of belief as there are those who believe.

BELIEVE IT OR NOT

One-legged giants toppled by a prehistoric monster

1

Introducing the Case of the Disappearing Atheists

A nightmare sometimes haunts my early waking hours. Dreaming I have just sat down to breakfast, I find next to my bowl of cereal the devastating headline staring up at me from the front pages of my daily paper.

CONSERVATIONIST SHOCK: EARTH'S LAST ATHEIST DISAPPEARS.

At first I cannot take in the implications of its frightening message, but then, as its full meaning gradually dawns, I shudder to think that all those atheists of my younger days are no more. What a terrible loss for dinner parties where once they could almost always be found murmuring godless witticisms in secluded corners of the room or crying out across the port about the esoteric implications of Schopenhauer, Nietzsche or Jean Paul Sartre. How we shall miss their radical pleas for justice on panel discussions once led by Robin Day, or their daring exploits into the theatre of the absurd. In many ways they were a kindly and amusing breed of *homo sapiens*, and the world will not be quite the same without them.

I wonder in my dream by what foul deed these atheists of former days suddenly met their end. Were they done in by unscrupulous treasure hunters collecting anthropological curiosities for the British Museum? Or could they have been destroyed by a change in the world's climate of opinion just as surely as the dinosaur was destroyed by a different sort of climatic change? Then again the solution to the mystery may be much simpler than I imagine. Perhaps they were simply knocked on the head by logical argument or cast to one side by wars and speculations more devastating by far than their own mild disbelief.

I may never know what really happened, but I do know that most of my nightmare has actually come true. For the atheists of former days have all but disappeared, even though their disappearance has not been noted by glaring headlines in the tabloid press. Gone are those heady days when H G Wells thought he had shown God His walking papers by creating his nightmare Utopia. No longer do we care that Huxley believed he had blasted God into oblivion with a scientific theory or Bertrand Russell with a mathematical formula. By now we are only mildly bemused to learn that George Bernard Shaw thought he had sent God to His eternal reward by discovering sin for the first time.

I well remember hearing people heatedly debate the propriety of burying an atheist like Shaw in the sacred precincts of Westminster Abbey, little realising at the time that they were already debating where to bury an entire age that had imperceptibly come to an end. No longer were we to see great herds of atheists stalking the earth, arguing for justice and equality and human rights. Gone also were the days when they might be found roaming through the lecture halls and drawing rooms of civilised society, carelessly destroying much of the very civilisation through which they roamed and knocking down the foundation stones of the very virtues they proclaimed; leaving in their wake poverty, despotism, and the orphanages of Romania as their only lasting memorial.

Departing with neither a bang nor a whimper, the old fashioned atheists just faded away into the mists of history, leaving behind them all those tyrannical governments built upon their weary philosophy which in turn have now been overthrown by a revolution of the human spirit no atheist could have ever foretold. In the end they proved a dangerous breed, yet I for one shall miss them. For, in spite of their destructive bent, they at least believed in something and were definite about what they believed. You could talk with an old fashioned atheist and know what you were talking about.

On those rare occasions when I have actually met a real atheist I have discovered that this ability to believe in something has given us much more in common than either of us would have ever imagined. When we argued with one another we knew where we stood for we both stood on the solid ground of faith. Whether my atheist friend was willing to admit it or not, we were long lost friends in the faith, differing only about the object of our faith. For though he could not believe in the existence of God, it was only because he so passionately believed in the goodness of Man. He placed his whole faith in humanity whereas I had come to place mine in divinity.

It was precisely his belief in humanity that kept him from believing in God. Unlike all those people today who think that religion is probably a very good thing but have no idea what it is really all about, the traditional atheist thought he knew exactly what religion was all about and he was convinced that it was about something so destructive of our humanity that it had to be stopped at all costs. He saw religion as mankind's worst enemy for it was built upon a tissue of lies which, though they might comfort some people for awhile, would, if allowed to remain unchecked, eventually stifle all human freedom and human progress.

This exclusive belief in humanity was the atheist's greatest strength, but alas it also led to his downfall. Those intellectual giants who strode across the Victorian landscape were all too often one legged giants. They placed all their weight on the goodness of man and none on the reality of God, so that eventually they toppled over from the very absurdity of their stance. In the court of rational argument their defence crumbled to the ground once the prosecution pointed out that most of the evidence suggested that mankind was not all that good. Events began to prove that once we no longer believe in God, there is very little reason for believing in mankind either - or in anything else for that matter. In proclaiming that God was dead the atheist ended up tolling his own funeral knell.

By trying to destroy God the atheist of former days only succeeded in destroying his own humanity, so that far from sending God into oblivion, he created an oblivion out of his own imagination that eventually became his own home. He met his end because he kept asking himself if God is real when he should have been asking himself what he meant by reality. What kind of world do we live in, and what is the meaning of life? What, for that matter, is the meaning of death and of evil and of suffering? Instead of proclaiming that as long as there is evil in the world he could not possibly believe in God, it would have been much more to the point for the atheist to have asked what kind of God, given all this evil, he could possibly believe in.

The atheist and I do not really disagree so much about the existence of God as about the kind of God we think exists. Even more to the point, the atheist seems thoroughly to misunderstand what kind of God I really believe in. He keeps shooting down straw men that I have not put up in the first place, and fails to realize that the kind of God he cannot believe in I cannot believe in either.

Like him, I cannot accept a God who is supposedly able to do anything He wants for mankind, but apparently does not care to do much of anything at all. Nor can I see any point in believing in a God who is either much too far away to be known by the likes of me, or much too like me to be worth knowing. I believe in a very different sort of God. I believe in a God who wants to do everything for mankind but is often unable to do so, and who is infinitely diffcrent from me but condescends to be very close to me as well. Unfortunately my atheist friend seems to have never heard of this kind of God, and instead chooses to believe in something like Humanity or Nature or Lady Luck, which, for some obscure reason, he finds more practical and down to earth than belief in the kind of God I believe in.

At least the atheist believed in these sort of things until Humanity and Nature and Lady Luck let him down so badly that by now he is no longer able to believe in much of anything at all.

Occasionally I think I see far off in the distance someone who still denies the existence of God in order to prove the goodness of Man. Following in the footsteps of such great protagonists for the Christian faith as C.S. Lewis or Dorothy L. Sayers, I run up with arm upraised eager to engage him in battle, only to discover, once I catch up with him, that he is nothing like the atheist I had expected to meet. Instead I find a rather vague and liberal agnostic who seems to have no real interest in proving or denying anything at all, unless perhaps it is to convince me of the rather obvious fact that there is serious starvation abroad and racial injustice at home.

Unlike the old-fashioned atheist these new liberal agnostics usually wish Christianity well, but it never occurs to them that it might actually be true, for they are much too cynical to believe that anything is necessarily true. Whereas I could once argue with a militant atheist and we both know what we were arguing about, I find it almost impossible to argue about anything at all with this new breed of unbeliever. Indeed, having abandoned all logical debate, he takes his stand on little more than his own individual feelings supported by the weight of public opinion.

The old committed atheist was able to stand his ground, but the new agnostic stands on constantly shifting ground. I start talking to him about the existence of God and he wants to know why some self professed Christians get into trouble with the police. In response I begin to explain temptation and sin, only for him to ask how a good God can allow so much evil in the world. Like Alice in Wonderland chasing the White Rabbit, I try to keep up with him by attempting to talk about love and free will and the devil, but before I have gone much beyond a few sentences he suddenly interrupts to say that if the church taught people to love one another we wouldn't need the police. Just when I thought I might be getting somewhere I find that I am right back where I started from. In trying to find some common ground with my protagonist he keeps throwing sand in my eyes, only for me to discover that suddenly, by some mysterious sleight-of-hand, the sand in my eyes has turned into quicksand under my feet.

More often than I care to recall I have allowed myself to be led into this quicksand of irrational debate, not by the strength of someone else's arguments but by the lack of any consistent arguments on which either of us can take a stand. The sinking feeling that comes over me makes me pray with all my heart that my protagonist may come to take a stand on some sort of solid ground no matter what, and that he may become committed to some sort of belief before both of us end up being committed to some institution instead.

This cynical fear of committing oneself to any kind of belief is far from typical of the average Englishman who has always been remarkably tenacious in his beliefs. You are much less likely to encounter such cynicism when talking to ordinary people on the street than when visiting the secluded cells of certain half-hearted, middle-aged clergy and professional theologians who seem to be constantly apologising for what little belief they still have left. Because they talk as though the case against atheism has still to be proven, they are, if not the cause, at least the perpetrators of a more universal scepticism which prevents the average man on the street from pursuing his natural quest for God and his search for truth.

I doubt that these quasi professional agnostics will like this book very much. But then it was not written for them, but for all those who are seeking a way out of the despondency of current doubt that has followed in the wake of an atheism now hopelessly out of date. It was written for all those modern sceptics now crowding the streets of our towns and cities who, contrary to their natural inclination, are afraid to believe in anything at all.

Most people I know desperately want to believe in something but are haunted by the taunts of imaginary atheists they neither know nor understand. The streets are crowded with people who have had some kind of genuine interest in the Christian faith but have done nothing about it for fear of being cut down or ridiculed by arguments beyond their grasp. They imagine that at every turn some atheist is lurking nearby ready to pounce on anything they might start to believe.

Death takes the son of my next door neighbour and for the first time in his life he makes a valiant attempt to pray. As we all learned in the last two world wars, there are no atheists in foxholes, and my neighbour sadly discovers that there are none at the grave side either. But then he hears some imaginary atheist laughing in his ear and quickly gives up his prayers as so much childish nonsense. At best he consoles himself by thinking that even though prayer does not do any real good it at least made him feel better for awhile.

Then there is the young girl who starts going about with Christian friends and begins to go to church. She enjoys what she finds and eventually becomes baptised and confirmed, only to be teased by her school mates and told by her parents that if she was such a good Christian she would help more around the house. The imaginary atheist begins to loom large before her and she stops going to church for fear of being thought a fool.

A man in his mid twenties or early thirties rejects the middle class values of his friends and parents. Looking about for something more important in life than a well paid job and a bigger house in the suburbs, he decides to let his hair grow long and begins to grow a rather scruffy looking beard. Perhaps he tries his hand at the guitar with some new amateur rock group. He may even dabble in the occult or start to explore some esoteric form of Eastern mysticism. The one thing he will never think of trying is Christianity. For our imaginary atheist drove that possibility out of his head once and for all almost as soon as he was born. Why, after all, pursue what everyone already knows was discredited long ago?

In what follows I have tried to provide some sort of antidote to this general atmosphere of religious scepticism which the old fashioned atheist has left in his wake. In doing so I have not attempted to offer every conceivable reason for believing in Christianity, but have only described those reasons which have persuaded me to believe as I do. Rather than trying to argue anyone into Christian belief, I have only wanted to reassure people that it is alright to believe. I am sure that reassurance rather than argument is what is needed today, and that this reassurance is more likely to come from a clear description of the Christian Faith than from a wealth of arguments in its favour.

New ways of thinking do not come easily to most of us. Unlike St Paul my own beliefs did not come in a single blinding flash of insight, but only after considerable study and long periods of quiet reflection. Yet even though the full weight of the reasons for believing in Christianity sank very slowly into my mind, I did not travel along the road of faith unaided. A great many people, including several authors who had made a journey similar to my own, helped me on my way, clarifying my own thinking just when I was becoming most unsure of the road I was attempting to follow. Because some of my readers may also find their writings helpful as they pursue their own spiritual pilgrimage, I have listed a few of them at the end of this book as suggestions for further reading.

When I first began to explore the Christian Faith I encountered ideas so strange that they seemed like nothing so much as terrifying monsters from some alien world. In bewilderment and confusion I shied away from them until the liberal agnostic convinced me that these newfangled ideas were nothing more than the fossilized bones of a prehistoric monster, and that what had seemed so strange and awesome in my first encounter were little more than museum pieces of only slight historical interest. With this reassurance my original fear turned into casual curiosity, and next my curiosity turned into familiarity. Then something completely unexpected happened. To my utter surprise I found that these new ideas, far from being antiquated remains of an extinct Christianity lying on the shelf in some museum, had almost unconsciously come to provide the very backbone of my everyday thinking and experience. What I had been told was a prehistoric monster turned out to be a very contemporary friend, ever giving me new confidence as I continued along the road of Christian belief. I learned that with ideas as with people, familiarity can breed reassurance rather than contempt.

If I have provided any such reassurance I shall be more than satisfied, bearing in mind that what follows is little more than a skeleton of one man's personal belief. No book and no amount of talk can provide absolute proof of anything. They certainly cannot prove the object of faith. Personal conviction needs the support of rational argument but it only comes from personal experience. As with the proverbial pudding, the proof of any argument lies always in the eating.

BELIEVE IT OR NOT

A cosmic pig catches unicorns unawares

2

A Plea For Scepticism

When I go to our new supermarket I am very rarely tempted to hit the check-out girl over the head. Though we are complete strangers, I am pleased to say that most of our differences are settled quite amicably. If, for example, I purchase eight pounds worth of groceries and she gives me a pound change for a ten pound note, I only need to point out the mistake and, with an apologetic smile, she hands over an extra pound. Someone looking on might easily assume that we were long-standing friends who, over the years, had built up an amazing amount of trust in one another. But of course I know that this friendly way of doing business really has nothing to do with friendship, but depends upon a commonly held belief in justice and a mutually shared conviction that two and two make four rather than five. Without even thinking about it, we both assume that I ought to be treated fairly and that eight from ten are not one but two.

What an amazingly clever and easy way to keep the peace! By a simple device of arithmetic combined with a sense of justice, brawls are avoided in supermarkets and riots in the streets. I sometimes wonder who could have held such sway over the minds of men that even to this day such complete strangers as the check-out girl and myself willingly sacrifice our own free thought to such impersonal and abstract standards of arithmetic and justice just for the sake of keeping the peace. Who convinced us that peace is really worth more than a pound in change?

Not everyone is convinced of course. Some people quite willingly break the peace for the sake of their own private gain. Dashing into supermarkets, often with guns pointed at cashiers and customers, they take what we believe is not rightfully theirs. And others, more subtle or less adventurous, try to make eight and one equal ten by fiddling the books. Yet even they are always peering over their shoulder lest they are caught, for they know that though we may at times admire their audacity, we never congratulate them for their honesty. Because they have stolen other people's goods, we universally agree that it is quite right for them to be hauled up before the magistrates and given their just reward.

Sometimes in my imagination I picture a single capital of the world where, in the central square, a great statue has been erected in honour of that unsung hero who first laid the cornerstone of this civilised behaviour by inventing the principles of arithmetic and justice. Or perhaps a brass plaque has been placed in his honour next to the tomb of that unknown warrior who gave up his life to ensure that this civilised behaviour might continue to live.

But on reflection I know that my imaginary statue will never be built nor any new plaque placed in Westminster Abbey. For there never was any such person. No one invented the basic principles of arithmetic simply to keep peace in supermarkets. Nor do we punish a man who invents his own arithmetic just because he endangers the peace or rebels against some arbitrary social custom. We punish him because we believe that in some sort of mysterious way his behaviour goes against the very nature of things. Whether we like it or not, we accept the principles of arithmetic as facts which every good willed person must obey and which all ignore to their peril. And what is true of arithmetic is also true of justice and fairness and all sorts of other good things like honesty and honour and mutual respect for one another. We believe that all these things should be encouraged simply because they are good in themselves, and that injustice and dishonour should be condemned. Even the criminal who holds up the supermarket submits to the basic facts of arithmetic, rarely if ever defending himself by arguing that two and two really do make five. It would seem after all that there really is honour even among thieves.

Perhaps, however, all this belief in honour and justice and arithmetic is mere superstition - a carry over from more primitive times when the human spirit was confined by the shackles of ignorance and prejudice. If so, should we not rise up in protest and allow the individual that wild and exotic freedom to proclaim, if he so wishes, that two and two really do make five? While we are at it, why not give him the right to believe in dishonour and injustice as well? Instead of condemning those who rebel against society's common beliefs, perhaps their defenders ought to be hauled into court to produce evidence that the principles of arithmetic really are true and that justice really is good.

Surely we have progressed to the point where we can be sceptical about all our social attitudes and question every common belief. Now that we are no longer afraid of black cats or black neighbours, nor look for Hallowe'en witches and hippie goblins round every corner, why not drive out once and for all every other remnant of ignorant superstition as well? Just as we were once mistaken about the mischievous antics of cats and witches which we thought we could see, are we not now much more likely to be mistaken about the goodness of justice and honour and mathematics which no-one can see? Having rid the world of one kind of superstition, let us rid the world of these other perfidious superstitions as well. Let our patron saint be Doubting Thomas who summed up our scepticism once and for all when he proclaimed: "Unless I feel the print of the nails in his hands and feet and put my hand in the hole in his side, I will not believe".

Sound the battle cry! Down with all unproven assumptions and death to every common belief for which we can find no evidence! I call all men of good will to join me in this battle against justice and arithmetic and every other kind of dogmatic belief that tramples underfoot our personal freedom. Yet despite my protestations, I find that few seem willing to take up the call. For when it comes to the most important issues of life, even the modern sceptic turns out to be as dogmatic as everyone else.

But then I suppose we must all be dogmatic about something, even if it is only about our own scepticism. Dogmas after all are really nothing more than the basic principles we take for granted as so obviously true that we rarely if ever need to think about them. Instead they provide the means for thinking about everything else and the foundation stones of our common life. Without them civilisation as we know it would come to an end. Seriously question the basic assumptions of mathematics and the natural sciences will collapse. Undermine our common belief in economic justice and half the world will starve. Deny a belief in the basic goodness of mankind and we will end up with social violence. Seriously doubt our own innate goodness and we will become suicidal.

It would seem that we can only build up some kind of integrated mental and emotional life on a foundation of facts and values which we do not have to prove because we believe that their truth is self evident. Without these self evident truths or dogmas there could be no sensible conversation, no advance in our thinking and no peace with our fellow men. They give us a place to stand and a court of appeal by which we can settle our differences. They bind us together in a universe of discourse and community of action without which there would only be chaos and disintegration both in society and in the individual.

Should people criticise my work I will either work harder or give up working altogether, but if they criticise my very right to work, I will immediately stand up for my rights. If they laugh at my clothes I can bear it, but if they strip me naked I will run away in embarrassment. I can even accept that my thinking may be wrong or that it may be foolish for me to die for my country, but I cannot accept that I am wrong because I think or that patriotism in itself is foolish.

The right to work and the need to be clothed as well as the importance of patriotism and freedom of thought are all part of the dogmatic furniture of my life which I must defend to the death. Such things make me what I am and in defending them I will even resort to violence if necessary, for I know intuitively that they cannot be defended by rational argument alone. There is no argument against the nudist or the person who chooses not to work, nor can I argue someone out of his prejudices if he refuses to think, nor encourage him to die for his country if he has no sense of patriotism. As with the cashier in the supermarket, all I can do if I am going to get my way is hit him over the head, and in similar fashion a society can only maintain its way of life by getting rid of all those who threaten its common assumptions.

To secure the peace every society must burn its heretics in either a literal or figurative way. People are imprisoned or hounded by the press. Others suffer more brutal practices. In Africa, South America and Asia many are murdered or disappear. In the middle ages, when our dogmas were mostly theological, the State, with the connivance of the church, burned its religious heretics at the stake. Now that we have given up the practice we wonder how a church could succumb to such an evil. But this is only because our own dogmas are no longer theological but economic and political, so that even though we are now free to choose our religious allegiances, no matter how bizarre, we are not free to choose our style of government in a world where capitalist democracy has become the final court of appeal for settling all our differences. King Demos has replaced the God of the ancient Jews as the foundation of our common life, and we must burn all those who threaten his supreme reign. Though we would no longer dream of burning theological heretics at the stake, Americans in the 1950s felt no compunction in burning the Rosenburghs in the electric chair for betraying the secrets of a capitalist democracy to the communists.

There is, however, a dogmatic ideology holding sway over our lives so much greater than our economic and political dogmas that no-one ever dreams of betraying its secrets or of undermining its absolute authority. Just as theology was once the science which supported the teaching and practise of church and state, so now we assume that "Science" itself and the scientific method are able to explain everything from religion to social behaviour and individual psychology. To question the pronouncements of science is to attack the very foundation of modern life.

Some years ago, when my son and I were crossing the English Channel, I started to point out to him, as we looked out towards the horizon, why the earth was obviously flat, whereas he kept insisting, in spite of all the evidence to the contrary, that the earth had to be round. It seemed at the time an innocent enough conversation until suddenly a lady in a forward deck chair, who apparently could stand it no longer, turned upon me with looks to kill. I am quite sure she would have turned her looks into action there and then if she had had the means and the courage. For I was obviously a dangerous public enemy who, like Socrates in ancient times, was guilty of perverting the youth and disturbing the peace by undermining the very basis of our common life.

She was right of course to appreciate all the marvellous benefits that the scientific method has given us, but she failed to realize that we get ourselves into trouble when we become dogmatic about everything that goes by the name of science or assume that all our scientific reasoning is reasonable. Like every other human activity scientific knowledge rests upon certain basic assumptions which cannot themselves be proven by reason. They must be accepted dogmatically and then tested by experience to see if they make sense and help us make sense of everything else.

My emotional stability depends upon all the innumerable beliefs I have always taken for granted, and should some of them stop making sense a terrible and often violent struggle develops within me. If their self evident truth no longer seems so self evident, I feel as though the rug has been pulled out from under my life and that the world I have built for myself is collapsing around my head, making me too paralysed either to think or to act responsibly. Until I can find new and more appropriate dogmas the meaning and purpose of life are swept away.

This sometimes happens with the death of our parents. In spite of all the evidence, most people assume that their mothers and fathers will live forever, for we have been taught from our childhood that it would be morbid to think otherwise. Then the day comes when bitter experience forces us to accept that parents really do die along with everyone else, and to the grief of our personal loss is added the almost unbearable pain of disillusionment as our original certainties are laid to rest in our parents' grave.

For many people today it seems as though few of their original certainties can still stand the test of actual experience. From the time they first discovered that there is no Father Christmas, one false dogma after another has come crashing to the ground until gradually their self-confidence has given way to disillusionment and they have learned to accept the bitter truth that no one can be trusted. Feeling terribly betrayed they are likely to hold their forefathers up to ridicule for having lied to them not only about their parents but about everything else as well. For the sake of their own personal survival they doubt everything they have ever been told and become cynical about every dogmatic belief they have ever held.

What is true of the individual is also true of society as a whole. All those dogmatic beliefs which once provided the corner stone of our culture are now open to doubt and subject to question. Our cultural myths have themselves become little more than pleasant stories from a more ignorant past. They may still point to a valuable moral but can never reveal the truth. Deprived of its dogmatic foundation our social stability can no longer be taken for granted. Peace is overcome by violence and every form of community life is threatened by individual self interest.

With all our traditional dogmas under threat, we have adopted an extreme sceptical stance, but paradoxically this has only made us more dogmatic than ever before. In a sceptical age we are not only dogmatic about our scepticism but about most everything else as well. Thinking we take nothing for granted, we have ended up taking most everything for granted and are in constant danger of falling victim to every kind of propaganda and pressure of public opinion.

Our convictions no longer rest on the truth of what is said but on our impression of who says what. Even though doctors constantly come up with new ideas about what is good for us, we place ourselves in their hands as though their latest opinions were infallible. New health diets come on the market almost every day, and yet we eagerly latch onto the latest one as though it was the final solution to all our problems. When scientists develop new theories we call it progress, rarely doubting that their latest theory is the correct one. Far from being genuinely sceptical we have simply substituted fads for principles, media "hype" for rational argument, and the proclamations of experts for scientific evidence.

The ancient pagans were far more sceptical than we are. Whereas we take each morning for granted because we assume that it is in the very nature of things for the sun to rise whether it likes it or not, every morning the pagans thanked their gods for making the sun rise once again because they did not think it really had to happen. Likewise, we who assume that justice and honour are too obviously right to be discussed on any occasion, are amazed to discover that the Greek philosopher Plato actually entertained his guests at dinner parties by making them puzzle out the reasons for believing in such things. Being superstitious dogmatists rather than philosophical sceptics, we would almost certainly find such dinner conversation extremely boring if not utterly boorish, much preferring the magical puzzles of Paul Daniels to the philosophical puzzles of Plato.

What was true of ancient philosophy was also true of science. The ancient Greek was quite capable of inventing the steam engine, but though he enjoyed playing with it as a toy, it never occurred to him to put hundreds of people behind the engine and carry them across the country. He was fascinated with the way the steam engine demonstrated his belief in certain principles of physics, but he never assumed that the principles which worked today would necessarily work tomorrow.

We need look no further than to our own children to find this same thorough going scepticism. Because, like Plato of old, they take nothing for granted, our children are forever bothering us with their interminable questions: "Why does water run downhill and why are trees green?" "Why do birds fly south in winter and why does the sun shine only in the day-time?" To which, in the midst of our over wrought lives, we give them the same reply day after day: "Well darling, they just do." Or perhaps, if we are very conscientious parents, we take time out to tell them about the law of gravity or the chemistry of chlorophyll. We may even let them in on the secrets of animal instinct or, if we think they are old enough, explain the rudiments of the solar system. But to our surprise, once we start explaining these things it becomes the child's turn to be bored, for when he asks why things are as they are, he does not want to know how things behave, but that it is right for them to behave the way they do. He is not asking for a lesson in physics but in philosophy.

Children take nothing for granted because they are interested in the truth about everything. We who have been blinded by our own unconscious dogmatism find it almost impossible to understand what they are on about. Having already decided what questions our children ought to ask and what explanations they should accept, we answer questions that are of no interest to them and offer explanations that explain nothing. What, after all, does instinct tell them about birds except that we have no idea why they fly south in winter, and what is gravity except a shorthand way of saying that everyone, like the child, has noticed that water runs downhill? Instinct and gravity and a host of similar things are modern myths we use to explain the unexplainable. They are mysterious gods we drag in for fear of falling into the abyss of mystery; dogmas we cling to in the blind hope of filling the gaps in our understanding of a mysterious universe.

Children will do everything they can to protect themselves from the onslaught of their parents' dogmas. When little Mary comes home and says she has just seen a lion in the next road she is expressing the fear and awe she feels when she leaves the security of her immediate neighbourhood. But if her father keeps insisting that there are no lions in the next road, the lion Mary saw will suddenly spring to life with a real mane and a frightening roar, whose existence she will defend even to the point of going to bed without her supper. She knows that her experience of the lion is real and that, for the sake of her own integrity, she dare not kill him off no matter how much pressure is put upon her by her parents. She has the wonder of St Peter when he wrote, "Be sober, be vigilant, for your adversary the devil walks about as a roaring lion seeking whom he may devour".

Yet even a child's wonder cannot be defended forever. From every television show that we allow our children to watch and from every book we encourage them to read, from their own parents and from most of their teachers, our children are daily bombarded with indefensible dogmas until finally they can withstand the pressure no longer. The lion eventually disappears, fear becomes repressed, and our children give up asking all the important questions. The healthy scepticism of a new generation is vanquished once again, and we adults can rest secure in a dogmatic and domesticated universe.

There is, however, still one area where scepticism reigns supreme, but where it is least appropriate. When it comes to religion in general and Christian belief in particular, the modern dogmatist remains such a thorough going sceptic that his scepticism often sounds more like uncritical cynicism. Though he expects his doctor to heal him, the most he expects of prayer is that it may make him feel better about being ill. In trying to sort out his personal problems he willingly goes to a psychiatrist, but treats priests as though they have nothing more to offer than personal opinions and private prejudices. When scientists come up with new theories about the universe he calls it progress, but when a theologian offers some new insight into the nature of God he calls it inconsistency.

The modern dogmatist avidly reads his horoscope but writes off the rapid rise in witchcraft and the occult as so much superstition. In tales of science fiction he eagerly pursues the wildest leaps of the imagination as though they might be true, but treats the idea of a virgin birth or bodily resurrection as too wild a fantasy to be entertained. Films like "E.T.", which authentically present the life of Christ under another name, become best sellers, and the traditional portrayal of the spiritual life in "Snow White and the Seven Dwarves" becomes a classic. But when it is pointed out that the story of the Extra Terrestrial Being is really the authentic story of the Christ of the Gospels and that Prince Charming is the Christian Saviour of the world who overcomes the deadly effect of the seven deadly sins, he dismisses these stories as so much childish nonsense. Having adopted the dogmatic scepticism of the day, he perversely turns to some fantastic and ill founded story like "The Last Temptation of Christ" to find out what Christianity is really all about.

Following the so-called "Age of Enlightenment", more than two hundred years ago, religion has been shunted into a siding of fantasy and irrelevance in the ungrounded hope that reason alone can solve all our problems. But unaided reason has failed to come up with the goods. The more we thought we knew, the more imponderable the universe became, until now reason itself has been pushed aside by our own irrational feelings.

Our faith in scientific reason has turned into an unscientific dogmatism, and the dream of a brave new world into a frightening nightmare in which the theoretical scientist has become a mad scientist and the practical scientist a technocrat whose achievements now threaten the very life of the planet and perhaps the existence of the universe. International attempts to rationalize politics have led to irrational war and violence whilst planned economies have brought starvation to much of the world. Analytical psychology has left nervous breakdowns in its train and battered children are the victims of a rationalised but impersonal social welfare.

Yet, with potential destruction all about us, a sceptical age still clings to its secular assumptions in the vain hope of finding salvation apart from God. We remain dogmatic about all that is vague and uncertain and unreliable, and question the only thing we can really be certain about.

Until now most everyone believed that if they were dogmatic about God they could be sceptical about everything else. They could fearlessly probe the meaning of every personal experience and question every social custom and human institution so long as they did not question the reality of God, for He alone gave them a place to stand from which they might move the world. Today, however, we cling to the most extraordinary beliefs that happen to come our way because we doubt the only truth that is absolutely true. Until we learn once more how to be dogmatic about God, we will never overcome our modern habit of jumping at every latest fad and taking every popular opinion for granted. If we are to find any worthwhile certainty in our lives, we must become sceptical of our society's misplaced scepticism and agnostic about our own ingrained agnosticism.

We can be certain about the reality of God because God is reality itself. If I am out rambling with my friend on a bright Sunday afternoon and suddenly call out: "Look, there is an amazingly fat pig in the next field", he as likely as not will follow my gaze in the hope of beholding the wondrous sight of an unusually round pink creature with a cut off nose at one end and something very much like an over sized pin curl at the other. Should I however exclaim instead, "See the beautiful unicorn in the next field", my friend is more likely to gaze into my eyes than into the field, doubting my integrity or my sanity.

Both of us know what a unicorn is and we have a fairly good idea what we mean by a fat pig, but, whereas experience and the stories of others have led us to believe that fat pigs really exist, the claim that a unicorn may exist raises a new and astounding idea which goes contrary to all our previous experience and teaching. It could, of course, be the other way round. I can easily imagine that on this or some far flung planet there are fields filled with unicorns but without a fat pig in sight. Search as much as I will, I might be forced to conclude that I live in a universe of unicorns where fat pigs are nothing more than a rather delightful but eccentric figment of my own imagination, for there is, after all, nothing about my idea of fat pigs, or of unicorns for that matter, which requires them to exist. I can imagine that they exist, but by doing so I cannot make them exist.

But even though I dare not be dogmatic about the existence of pigs or unicorns, I have to be dogmatic about the fact that some things do exist, and that even though nothing need be real there is such a thing as reality. I must, at the very least, be dogmatic about the reality of a mind which can imagine the existence of unicorns, and even if I should be nothing more than a speck of dust on the floor imagining the universe, I must still be dogmatic about the existence of the speck.

I must face the fact that Being simply is, that Reality is real, and that Existence exists. Though the truth seems so obvious as to be little more than a platitude hardly worth mentioning, once it is said we are plunged into realms too profound to be grasped by our small minds and too mysterious to be understood. The very mystery of the universe is revealed and the depths of all our experience probed, for by discovering the obvious we come face to face with none other than God Himself.

In our misplaced scepticism we have too easily forgotten that to be dogmatic about the reality of God is only to be dogmatic about reality itself. Even the old fashioned atheist believed in a reality totally independent of what he thought about it, and he desperately wanted to know what it was like. He fought for truth because he passionately believed there was such a thing as truth, for it was not Reality that the atheist denied but only a previous generation's image of Reality. He did not really deny the existence of God, as he thought, but only the God of his forefathers.

Today however most people neither agree nor disagree with their forefathers, because they are no longer interested in the meaning of existence nor in the nature of reality. When little Joey asks why water runs downhill or why trees are green he is on a spiritual quest searching into the depths of the mind and heart of God. But when he hears only answers that answer nothing, he abandons his quest and, ceasing to wonder at the mystery behind the appearances of things, the certainty of God dies within him. He loses his natural capacity for wonder and learns to get on with life as best he may. Unlike the former atheist he does not deny the existence of God but simply loses all interest in the question. He has become a modern sceptic and ends up being a dogmatic sceptic who no longer denies or questions anything at all.

Because today's sceptic does not believe in anything very deeply, he never questions anything very seriously. Having lost all interest in God, he falls prey to every god he encounters, whether it be the demonic gods of success and security, or the benevolent but seemingly powerless gods of justice, peace and general goodwill. Believing in nothing with any certainty, he accepts everything without question and falls prey to every esoteric fashion that comes along, be it drugs or transcendental meditation, LSD or CND, hooliganism, fascism or feminism, vegetarianism or genetic engineering. Any of these may prove good or bad in themselves but he has no way of knowing because he has no place where he can take a stand on anything whatsover. His very doubts about the reality of God have made him a devotee of all the gods.

BELIEVE IT OR NOT

Challenging the gods

3

THE BATTLE OF THE GODS

I did not grow up believing in the gods. Few if any of our generation did. From what little we knew the gods were nothing more than rather foolish supernatural fantasies invented by denizens of a more ignorant age either out of fear of the unknown or to control others even more ignorant than themselves. But whatever their origin our generation believed that the gods had been killed off centuries before and certainly had no place in the modern mind. Only when I was much older did I come to discover that the ancient gods were far from dead and anything but foolish. I had simply failed to recognize them, because ever since I was born, they had been walking through my life disguised as nothing more than everyday things and very ordinary people.

I no longer remember the exact moment when I first encountered the gods. At the time I was far too young to remember much of anything at all. But I think it may have happened when I began to sense that my mother was a potential enemy who might someday take away my life support system, or that the bars of my crib were a prison house designed by some insidious power to curtail my freedom. Perhaps the gods revealed themselves for the first time when my legs buckled out from under me and the floor, in some sort of perverse desire to punish me, rose up and struck me in the face. All I know is that at some such traumatic moment I became vaguely aware of innumerable forces impinging upon my life which the ancient pagans simply called "the gods" but which modern secularists call nothing at all.

In the womb I was neither aware of myself nor of anything other than myself, but once I was born I was thrown into a world quite indifferent to my most basic needs. My new world seemed filled with forces that for some unknown reason had it in for me. All sorts of objects objected to my every wish. Hard implacable gods were indifferent to even my most innocent desires and ready to punish every offence. Here were gods who needed to be conquered or at least controlled; gods to be appeased or cajoled into helping me fulfil my dreams. With ancient peoples I discovered that we live with forces much greater than ourselves, whimsical, arbitrary and often vindictive forces that we must at least try to win over to our side and perhaps even turn into friends. With the wise old teacher from the epic film *Star Wars* I echoed in my heart the universal prayer of all humanity: "May the Force be with you".

With that semi-conscious prayer my own religious quest began, though at the time I had no idea there was anything religious about it. Isolated in the midst of an alien world and surrounded by mysterious gods I could not name, I set about to find peace in an enemy territory and companionship in a hostile land. I sought that deep inner peace which only much later I learned was common to all religions, no matter how diverse or even bizarre the quest may have sometimes been. I sought that peace which the ancient Jews called "shalom" and the Navaho Indians "hozro", that undifferentiated "nirvana" of the Buddhist where all alienation comes to an end, that perfect balance of "yin" and "yang", or light and darkness, desired by the Chinese, that peace which "passes all understanding" said to be offered to the faithful Christian.

Once I began my search I discovered to my surprise, even as a child, that not all the gods were hostile. Sometimes I found friendship where I least expected it and love when I needed it most. The grown-ups in my life were not only gods to be feared but potential friends who, in several ways, were very similar to myself, reflecting like a many faceted mirror the various aspects of my own complex personality. Even my parents who drew from me a strange combination of awesome respect and genuine affection were surprisingly very similar to me, thinking much the way I thought, dreaming dreams like mine, and, like me, making up their own minds about what they wanted to do. What was true of my parents was also true of all the other people I knew and to some extent of everything else as well. I lived in a world shot through with signs of my own personality where everything struck certain cords of recognition within me.

I liked my neighbour's dog because there was something about him very much like me. He too could run about and play and obey my commands, just as I had to obey my parents' commands. And as I loved the dog who did my bidding, so I envied the lion who had more power than I or even than my parents, and I sometimes wondered what it would have been like to have been born a lion instead of a little boy. Even roses and Brussels sprouts showed some of the signs of life I found in myself, and the very stars shone with a glory similar to my own dreams of glory. Rocks and rivers had a stability and dependability I looked for in myself. Yet there was also something missing in everything around me. Parents and other grown-ups, no matter how much like me they sometimes seemed, actually lived in a world very different from my own. And even though my neighbour's dog was in some ways a companion closer to me than my parents could ever be, I could never converse with him about my hopes and fears. The Lion's power was greater than mine by far, but I also had a power I could never share with him, for I could argue to my heart's content about the rights and wrongs of eating people and he had no way of answering back. In Walt Disney fantasies all the animals might be my friends, but in real life I found that we continued to be alienated from one another in all the things that mattered most.

What was true of animals was true of everything else as well. Roses and sprouts, though alive, could neither sit up and beg for food nor run to me when I called, and there was no way that stars and stones, with neither breath nor life, intelligence nor freedom, could ever offer me the companionship I so desperately desired. Though I could kick the stone that skinned my knee as often as I wished it made absolutely no difference to the stone, for no matter how violent my attack, it neither loved me nor hated me but simply remained a stone.

In spite of all the ways in which my world of stones and stars, sprouts and dogs, fathers and mothers was so much like myself, there remained a great gulf between us which no power on earth seemed able to bridge. That perfect peace I sought seemed always just beyond my grasp.

I held out a hope that the time might come when I would meet someone who would completely understand me and give me all the support I needed. Perhaps it would be a girl friend or my future wife and children. It might even turn out to be one of my closest friends. So I thought, but it was not to be, for though I now have several close friends and a very understanding wife who has given me five lovely children, none of them completely understands me. Sometimes they seem very understanding, but this usually happens when just about everything is alright anyway. It is when I feel that I desperately need their support that they almost always let me down. And I suppose this should not really surprise me, for they cannot possibly give me all the support I need because they need all the support they can get from me. They are not gods but human beings like myself with the same loves and fears and cares that I have. I was asking of them what only the gods can give and the burden was too great for them to bear.

I love my wife with affection, but I am driven to worship the gods out of fear and awe. I fall to the ground in abject adoration before all the forces assaulting me from every side because they are greater than I and beyond my control. I am alienated from them and my alienation compels me to worship. Though some may think that there is a spark of the divine in every boulder and in every speck of sand, only the mountain looming over me and seemingly indifferent to my safety demands my subservient respect. Far from making either God or the gods in our own image, we only worship those things we cannot make over into our own image nor force to serve our own interests. The honour due to the gods is only given to those forces and creatures which are independent of our own ambitions and must be cajoled momentarily into doing our bidding. Once we learn to control the mountains which may erupt at the slightest provocation. or domesticate the animals we find in the wild, we no longer worship them as gods but enjoy them as companions existing for our own pleasure or as slaves to fulfil our every whim. By turning animals into pets and mountains into package holidays we secularize the sacred and make the world safe for pursuing our own pleasure.

The ancient Egyptians worshipped the sun because their life depended upon it, and the Assyrians worshipped the moon because, as they were quick to point out, the sun only shone when it was already light. To the Greeks and Romans it seemed obvious that the god of the storm, whether he be Zeus or Jupiter, was king of all the gods, for all life and death depended upon him. And among human beings, kings and heroes more powerful than themselves were easily treated as children of the gods. The pagan soldier at the foot of the cross paid Jesus a great compliment, but he did not experience some sudden conversion, when he exclaimed, "Truly this was the son of a god". So after all was Caesar.

In my search for peace I may try to secularize an alien world by winning it over to my side and killing off its hostile gods, living in the hope that eventually I will bring everything under my control, but in my heart of hearts I know that the hope must forever remain a vain hope, for the gods are not so easily domesticated nor so casually destroyed. Demanding my subservient worship they forever remain arbitrary and deceitful, lustful, selfish and aggressive.

I make promises and offer sacrifices to the storm god, only to have my house struck by lightning. I pray to the god of healing and my son still dies of cancer. I worship the god of love and the other gods are jealous. They cannot give me peace for they are themselves at war with one another, competing for my undivided attention and devotion. The demands of conscience, friends, family, church, job or school all pull me in opposite directions so that to fulfil my commitment to one is to betray another. If I give myself to political idealism, economic reality strikes me down. If I devote myself to my work, my wife and children feel rejected.

I have finally learned, like all those who have gone before me, that in one way or another we are engaged in a perpetual battle with hostile gods no matter how friendly some of them may seem. We must worship them in humble adoration and yet, if we are to survive, we must also protect ourselves from their attacks. I remember how even in the earliest days of my religious quest I developed certain techniques to keep these hostile gods at bay, learning as a child a few magic incantations like "eenie, meanie, miney, moe", and adopting a few simple rituals such as never stepping on cracks in the pavement or keeping a rabbit's foot or some other talisman in my pocket.

In themselves these were little more than games I played to prove that I could walk the streets in safety. Far more complex weapons were developed by our forefathers in their battles with the gods. Sacrificial rites and methods of meditation, scientific knowledge and political power, works of artistic imagination and the pursuit of financial security have been but a few. But ultimately all of them fail, for sacrificial rites develop into grotesque forms of human sacrifice and meditation into drug induced forms of self destruction; scientific knowledge and political power become wed in the charred remains of Hiroshima, and artistic imagination is reduced to little more than a source of private wealth feeding an insatiable greed.

I found that rest from battle only came at those rare moments when I could indulge in daydreams uninterrupted. In my dreams of glory I alone was god and those other awesome and fearful gods surrounding me were turned into docile slaves forced to do my bidding. I was a god invading the inner sanctums of the enemy and making the world of my fantasies safe for myself and for my friends - or, as I became older, safe for democracy or tyranny, for justice or free enterprise or whatever other idealism happened to strike me at the time.

Years ago, during the Second World War, the American magazine, "The New Yorker" published a series of cartoons called 'Dreams of Glory'. One that has stayed in my memory showed a small boy about my age standing across from Hitler's desk with pistol in each hand and crying out triumphantly: "Stick 'em up!" in the best John Wayne tradition. Of such romantic material are those dreams of glory made which drive us forward and give us hope in the midst of personal failure. They offer us a fragile peace whilst we momentarily imagine that we have conquered the gods.

Yet, as I soon discovered, such dreams can prove extremely dangerous. Not only can they distract us from getting on as best we can with the business of living in the "real world" of everyday life. They also never really take away the pain of alienation suffered in that world, but just drive it deeper into the inner recesses of our minds. Sometimes, when the pain becomes too great to bear, we run away along the road of self destruction either by retreating back into the womb where we can forget ourselves altogether or by giving ourselves over to some kind of collectivist nirvana where nothing in itself is real. We give up the battle of this world and surrender to its gods. Yet even this is no strategic retreat nor any dream of glory, but only a dream of terror. In a nightmare of casual indifference and conformity to social pressure, we run the risk of losing our own personal identities forever. By retreating from the battlefield of the gods we endanger our own souls.

As Faust learned when he made a deal with the devil, the ultimate price any of us pay when we make peace with the gods is the destruction of our own humanity. For in our desire for peace we allow the enemy to pillage that distinctive personality which is the only thing we really have worth fighting for. Almost before we begin to fight we lose the battle of the gods and the enemy returns from the battlefield bearing all the trophies of victory in what any impartial observer must surely call an unjust war.

Final victory over the gods only comes in the dream worlds of Homer or Tolkien where the hero is eventually able to return to his native land in peace. Bilbo returns to The Shire and Ulysses goes back to Ithaca, and we would like to think that that is the end of the story and that once we have exposed all the Wizards of Oz and the other gods of this world, we can cry out with Dorothy, "There is no place like home." But, as the film *Star Wars* makes abundantly clear, it never turns out this way in real life. After our initial victory over the gods there is always a sequel. With Luke Skywalker we discover that the empire always strikes back, and in the tales of all those who have done battle with the gods we learn the bitter truth that every hero is a tragic hero and every victory a Pyrrhic one. As G.K. Chesterton once commented about the White Horse of the Berkshire Hills, and about the church and all other things worth keeping, "If you would have the horse of old, you must scour the horse anew." And in his epic poem acclaiming the victories of King Alfred, Chesterton wisely prophesied that when the king grows old and too weak to fight the barbarians will come again. The unending refrain resounds throughout the heavens: "I tell you nought for your comfort, yea nought for your desire, save that the sky grows darker yet and the sea rises higher."

This at least was the prophetic warning that rang down all the ages until our Victorian grandparents put a new twist to the old tales. In the dream world of Wonderland everything suddenly became personal, whimsical and arbitrary except for Alice herself. Rabbits now talk and hatters have gone mad but she has become a god of hard mathematical fact. Rationalism has won the day and men's new hope now lies in subduing the hostile gods of this world simply through unfeeling reason. By ignoring their own hearts' desires and adjusting their minds to the implacable laws of an impersonal world, our grandparents thought that the world itself could be reduced to their own tyrannical control. A new religion was born in which the scientific method became the only means of salvation, scientists became the new saints and the abandonment of personal dreams of glory became the new human sacrifice.

The early Fathers of the Christian Church reduced the ancient gods to impotent demons, but the Victorians went a step further and reduced them to unthinking objects and mere physical forces. Lightning was no longer king of the gods but only lightning, the stars became mere chunks of matter, and matter itself just an amalgamation of bundles of energy to be understood and controlled by men. At long last the gods were finally dead, having been killed off by nothing more than the deft stroke of the modern philosopher's pen.

Having tasted the blood of battle and with victory over the whole universe seemingly in our grasp, we did not stop at killing off the gods. Revelling in our grandparents' initial triumph over the gods of this world, we next learned to tread upon the face of the man in the moon and now look forward to bringing the very stars under our control. We reach out to destroy the gods of the entire cosmos but in the process we destroy the god-like character of ourselves as well. Writers attempt to explain the complexities of human behaviour by reducing us to naked apes, setting aside imagination and will and all those other things which make us uniquely human. Others reduce our minds to electrical impulses of the brain and then our brains to the mathematical calculations of the computer.

And in the philosophy of Behaviourism the last vestiges of human freedom are swept away, so that we who set about to control the universe have become nothing more than relatively insignificant components of a universal machine that runs on its own steam.

Not just our humanity but every other form of life has come under attack as well. Along with every other earthly creature the apes have been reduced to insignificant forms of protoplasm, and by now even the objective reality of the protoplasm seems to be in doubt, so that we no longer think we have to come to terms with anything outside ourselves. Objective truth and standards of goodness as well as the threat of evil are all brushed aside. Nothing is left for our schools to do but teach us how to express ourselves. As the poet said much earlier, nothing is right or wrong, nothing true or false, but thinking makes it so. Everything unique about us is destroyed, and all that is special and valuable in our world is gradually wiped away from the consciousness of men.

Now that we no longer believe in the gods we no longer believe in ourselves, so that lack of self confidence has become the disease of our day and depression its most devastating symptom. Without believing in myself I can believe in little else, for I am after all the only creature I can directly know. A creature who dreams and worries, makes decisions and acts either for good or ill, who knows certain things and knows that he knows, who breathes and feels pain, laughs and weeps, loves and hates, eats and sleeps, and is capable of being loved or betrayed. Only by enjoying the mystery of myself am I able to appreciate the mystery of everything else as well. I discover the whole universe through knowing myself, and through my own god-like qualities I recognize the gods. If then I should declare that the gods are dead, I have done little more than kill off my own soul. To will the destruction of the gods must always be our last will and testament, for once the gods have gone nothing more can happen. We may still walk the earth, but we walk as the living dead.

I grew up in this kind of godless and soul destroying world, though, as I have said, I eventually discovered that it was not near as godless as I had been led to believe. The world was really just as alien as it had always been and the ancient gods were far from dead, for we do not, as I learned, get rid of the gods simply by denying their existence but only disguise them so that they can go about their work unchallenged and undetected. Like everyone else in the history of the world I was born a pagan, but I was a pagan deprived of every magic rite, religious technique and inner resource for dealing with gods I neither knew nor recognized.

Our grandparents foolishly thought that by killing off all the gods they would make it possible for us to go about our business without being haunted by the superstitious fears of previous generations. But they have been proven terribly wrong. Because of them we grew up knowing nothing of the gods, but in our ignorance the empire of the gods has now struck back, and we who thought we had conquered the forces of this world have become the victims of the conquered. By trying to force everything in our environment to serve our own ends the environment itself has ended up threatening to destroy us and all earthly life as we have known it. Apparent victory over the gods has only succeeded in threatening the lives of the victors' children in an alien world where, as the ancient prophet once foretold, the fool alone cries out, "'peace, peace' when there is no peace".

When all is said and done the gods still reign supreme, and the world remains our potential enemy no matter how much we may try to tame it. Though we occasionally win spectacular victories over the world's gods, the victories are always short lived. If we set about to destroy the gods of the Amazon forest for our own private gain, the sky gods which control the weather will threaten to destroy all the forests of the earth. Should we then attack the sky gods for the sake of our own convenience, the atmosphere will escape from the earth until there will soon be no more air left to breathe. Delve into the very depths of the forces behind all the gods and "The Force" strikes us down. Crack the atom and the earth will burst asunder.

So long as this threat to human life did not directly threaten us we did not bother very much about it. There was in fact a certain political advantage in thinking of other people as little more than bundles of physical energy to be disposed of at will. Yet even that proved short lived, for though it was relatively easy for men to drop napalm on the forests of Vietnam if they were trained to think of their unsuspecting victims as mere blobs of protoplasm, the tables were turned when the protoplasm crossed the ocean to take refuge in their homes. It was as though these Vietnamese boat people had come from another planet or from some far-flung galaxy. Suddenly we discovered that we still live in a mysterious universe beyond our control. Just as we thought that physics and astronomy would give us the victory over ancient gods, presidents and their people began to rely upon the archaic science of astrology. Far from conquering the stars we began to place ourselves and our common destinies under the control of the stars and all the other mysterious forces of the universe. When we thought we had destroyed the gods, they returned as demons threatening to destroy their would-be conquerors.

I came to see that this has been the sad story of the twentieth century. In stripping Germany of all its power after the First World War we only succeeded in giving birth to Hitler. In destroying the ozone layer for our own convenience we are now in danger of being destroyed ourselves. Though we may have found some kind of common ground with our enemy by reducing ourselves and everything else to unthinking bundles of energy, the price we have paid is the destruction of the bodies and souls of men. By sacrificing our unique freedom and human personality we appear to be witnessing the end of life on earth as we have known it.

No wonder the heroes of the ancient tales are always tragic heroes, for in a world that cannot be controlled or changed by mere mortals, human life must always end in tragedy. It would seem that endurance rather than victory is the most we can hope for in our perpetual battle with the gods. The sensible man must either learn to keep a stiff upper lip with the ancient Stoics, or else join the Epicureans and "eat, drink and be merry, for tomorrow he will die".

If we are to win even the smallest victories over gods more powerful than ourselves, we must pursue the battle with true religious fervour and make use of all the religious techniques devised throughout the ages, even though the techniques themselves may eventually destroy us. Only those militants who treat established values as some kind of evil gods are able to fight religiously for disarmament or racial equality. Yet even their greatest achievements are short lived as the causes for which they fight are gradually absorbed into the established social and political system and their hippie leaders become heads of respectable corporations. Revolutionaries are always defeated by the religious fervour of their own revolutions. Though religious fervour may be necessary in fighting the gods, it will not help us avoid the mortal wounds of combat. Religion may be needed for survival but it can also prove very dangerous, as we discovered at the end of the seventies when, in obedience to a self-proclaimed messiah, a thousand people marched off to Ghana and drank from a vat of cyanide.

Some who are slightly less fervent in their attempt to resolve the conflict between themselves and hostile gods simply hand themselves over to some form of Satanic worship. But this too ends in failure. Hoping to overcome the gods of the established order, they worship all the demonic forces that go against commonly accepted standards of truth and decency, only to be gradually taken over by forces of evil beyond their control. They too eventually learn that the gods are no more easily removed from their thrones by the worship of evil than by the pursuit of goodness.

Though my own attempt to find peace and harmony in this world may at times have a certain tragic nobility about it, it must eventually end in certain failure. I may learn to use rocks and stones and other inanimate objects to suit my own interests, and to prune the roses, tame the lion and domesticate my neighbour's dog, yet I can never ultimately resolve the fundamental conflict of warring gods who I know will continue to do battle with one another and with the likes of me long after I am gone.

The battle of the gods continues no matter what any of us try to do about it. If I join the battle I always end up the loser, and if I try to remain outside the fray I become the innocent victim. In a vain attempt to escape such certain defeat I may try to run away from the battle altogether by retreating into myself or by burying myself in my work or perhaps by declaring myself an atheist. But there is no such easy escape from the gods, for they cannot be conquered simply by pretending they are not there. Perhaps the ancient philosophers were right when they saw this earthly body as a prison house from which our eternal soul has to escape. But, if so, then the only escape is death, and nobility is to be found only in suicide, honour in self-destruction, and peace in the obliteration of our own unique individuality.

With St Paul I cry out, "Who will deliver me from this death?"

BELIEVE IT OR NOT

Moses discovers the will of God

4

Public Revelations

If I am to be delivered from spiritual death I must somehow learn to live amongst the gods, whilst rising above their everlasting warfare. I must find a place to stand in the shifting sands of my own inner turmoil, so that I may begin a quest for an unknown god who will care for me and yet remain unscathed by the conflicting forces of this world, a unique god to whom I can somehow sacrifice myself without losing my own individual soul.

When I first began my search for such a god I was bombarded by a host of philosophies and religions all competing for my allegiance, and I could not imagine any way of deciding which one I ought to follow. I did not know whether to be a Platonist or a Marxist, a Buddhist or a Druid or perhaps a Christian Scientist, until I came to realize that most all of these competing philosophies and religions were only variations on a single theme. The vast majority limited everything, both human and divine, to our individual experience of life just as it is. For them the gods are nothing more than the personified forces of our everyday world. Though people of different cultures had different needs and required different religious responses to these needs, all assumed that the gods and the forces dominating their world were one and the same thing.

Just a few of these religious responses, however arose from the assumption that at the heart of our individual experience there is a God above all the gods who made the world out of nothing. He reigns supreme over all the forces dominating our lives and never gets enmeshed in the never ending wars of lesser gods. In my own desperate desire to escape the perpetual battles of the gods, this God beyond the gods seemed to deserve my most immediate attention.

Soon I discovered that those few religions and philosophies which believe in such a God all derive from the beliefs and practices of a single ancient tribe of Near Eastern nomads who lived nearly two thousand years ago. By turning to the ancient Jews it looked as though I might discover a God who actually cares about what happens to me and to the world in which I live. Perhaps with the Jews I would find a God I could revere without falling into the pagan trap of investing the world itself with divine personalities vying with one another for the ultimate control of my soul.

I found that the ancient Jew was no different from all the rest of us. Like myself and everyone else, he grew up with objects that objected to his own desires and with things and people that seemed to hold mastery over his life. Unlike the devout pagan or the modern sceptic, however he did not search for peace in the midst of these warring gods because it never occurred to him that the people and things with which he had to come to terms were actually divine. Behind the arbitrary catastrophes of daily life and all the fiery darts of outrageous fortune, behind the cold and indifferent fate that so often seems to rule our lives, he took in with his mother's milk the belief that there is only one Lord and Master of his life, and that peace is only to be found in obeying His will. The true God is above, beyond and outside all the conflicts of this world; He overrides or transcends our everyday experience and remains true to Himself in spite of every earthly trial. The ancient Jews, like all who have followed in their footsteps, believed they were safe from the warring gods of this world because they were saved by a God who is not of this world. As the Jewish Prayer Book always insisted, heaven is God's throne and earth is His footstool: "He dwells between the cherubim, be the earth never so unquiet".

The Jews did not always see things this way. Like the rest of us they started off assuming that there were all sorts of gods, the most powerful being the god of the storm and the god of the volcano. Just as the Greeks worshipped Zeus and the Romans Jupiter, so the Jews worshipped the same god under still another name, a god of cosmic power who became jealous if other gods were given too much attention. Like everyone else the Jews saw themselves as victims of warring gods until slowly they hammered out on the anvil of their common experience a unique insight into the mystery of the universe.

Something happened which shook the Jewish nation to its foundations and left an indelible mark on every Jew from that day to this. Something forced the Jews to realize that their god was not jealous because he was in competition with other gods but because he cared for them much too much to let any other god lead them astray.

They first began to think that this god really cared for them when Abraham believed that he was called out of his native town of Ur of the Chaldees to become the father of a great nation. It was as though for some mysterious reason their own tribal god had a special interest in Abraham and his children, and for awhile this was born out by all the victories they won against neighbouring hostile tribes. Then something suddenly went terribly wrong. They ended up as persecuted slaves in Egypt, and it seemed as though their god had abandoned them to the arbitrary whim of a foreign power beyond their control.

Then, when all hope seemed lost, Moses suddenly rose up out of the Nile to act as a go-between or mediator between the Jews and their god, and under his guidance god led his people out of Egypt and rescued them from certain death at the hands of Pharaoh's army. Fleeing the pursuing Egyptians they were saved from total destruction when the waters of the nearby marshes, lying as a barrier between themselves and the land promised them by their god, were blown aside by a strong East wind allowing them to cross in safety. Even so their final deliverance had not yet come, for when they looked back they saw to their horror the Egyptians relentlessly continuing their pursuit through the once watery marshes. They knew that only god could save them now, but little did they expect him to do precisely that. Whilst staring at the Egyptian soldiers desperately trying to dislodge their chariot wheels from the soft mud of the sea bed which they themselves had crossed just moments before, the wind suddenly died down and the enemy drowned in the rush of returning waters.

In such spectacular fashion they learned that their god reigned supreme over all the pagan gods. The tyrannical Egyptians perished in the quicksand of their pagan minds and the one true god led His chosen people, with a cloud during the day and a pillar of fire at night, through the wilderness of trials and temptations towards the promised land. Why the waters fled and what this fire and cloud may have been never much interested the Jews. For them the important thing was that their escape from slavery into freedom brought with it an amazing discovery. Because of this apparently miraculous deliverance the Jews came to believe that they worshipped the most powerful of all the gods. No longer some sort of personified force arbitrarily controlling their lives, their god had become a real person more powerful than all the forces of this world combined. Able to drive out the mighty gods of the Egyptians He alone was worthy to be called God, and for some inexplicable reason this personal and all powerful God had a personal interest in them.

Marching forward in this conviction they won victory after victory over all the nations surrounding them, and later over the powerful Greeks and Syrians who tried to drive them out of the land they believed God had given them. Their victories seemed to prove that "The Force" was personally interested in them and would save them from all the conflicting forces of pagan neighbours. God was on their side and would protect them from the onslaught of the gods.

To this very day, when a devout Jewish boy hears how God once saved his people from slavery in Egypt, his heart wells up within him, not out of nostalgia for an ancient story, but because the ancient story is so very modern. God's salvation of his people was not just a one off event, but an event that continues throughout the ages. Because God is consistent in everything He does, the devout Jew believes that if He saved His people once He will save them always. Because He once led His people into the promised land after years of persecution in Egypt, they could expect Him to lead them into a new State of Israel after the Holocaust of the Second World War. If at the beginning He created the world in six days, we need not be surprised that in the 1960s He re-created His people's freedom from Egypt in a "Six Day War".

The Jews believe they can depend upon their God to save them because He is not a God of arbitrary whim but one who knows His own mind. He is consistent in everything He does because He is at one with Himself. There is nothing schizophrenic about Him, no stresses nor strains within Him. Because He is not at war with Himself we can count on Him to do what He says.

The God of the Jews is a God of law and order and He has built order into the world He has made so that, in spite of all the changes and chances of life, we can also count on the world to behave in predictable ways. As the Jewish psalmist proclaimed, and the ancient pagan never understood: "He made the round world so sure that it cannot be moved at any time." Plague, fire and famine may be signs of His anger, but He is more clearly seen in the daily rising of the sun, for He is not so much known in the occasional miracle as in the dependability of cause and effect.

The Jews also discovered that you do not play around with a God of law and order unless you know the rules of the game. Here too the Jews believed that God had specially blessed them, for not only had He saved them from slavery in Egypt, but in the wilderness of temptation He had actually revealed his laws to Moses. High upon the mountain, in the midst of lightning, fire and resounding thunder, God had declared His mind, and the people learned that it is a fearful thing to fall into the hands of a living God who is also a God of unchanging and immutable law. This was no Sunday School lesson about decency and respectability but a terrifying experience that shook the Jews to the very depths of their souls. Yet they were forever grateful because the law also saved them from certain death and final destruction.

Knowledge of the law made it possible for the Jews to know what to do and what to avoid, just as my knowledge of the law of gravity keeps me from jumping out of windows in the upper floors of office buildings through the mistaken belief that I might go up instead of down. If I knew nothing about the law of gravity I would of course have no fear of open windows and with smiling equanimity could easily face up to anyone trying to push me out of one. Despite my blissful ignorance however, I would still go down instead of up, probably to my certain death. The Jew and I rarely if ever curse the day we came to know the law, for though our knowledge of the law puts serious constraints upon our freedom it also saves our lives.

The Jews believed that in an orderly world everything is governed by some law or other, and that only by respecting these laws would everything be alright. By honouring your father and mother and not going about killing your fellow Jews, your national energies would not be dissipated in blood feuds with your neighbours nor would your soldiers betray one another on the battlefield. And if you carefully cleansed all your pots and pans and avoided eating contaminated pork, your soldiers would not be constantly dropping dead from food poisoning. Most important of all, you would have something worth fighting for if you maintained your cultural identity by not getting mixed up with a lot of foreigners. You would save the soul of the nation by not marrying the daughters of aliens, nor worshipping their gods nor eating their strange exotic foods.

It was not the North American Blacks of the 1960s but the Jews thousands of years before who first discovered "soul food", which in their own language they called kosher. In discovering this soul food and all the other laws governing their every day lives they also discovered that they were free to go against these laws and eat foreign food if they so wished. They could become "Uncle Toms" by betraying their cultural inheritance and going against their national God. Because they knew the law they also knew how to break the law, and in this knowledge they found an amazing and exhilarating new insight about themselves that established their individual freedom forever and made them potential sons and daughters of God Himself. By tasting the tree of the knowledge of good and evil they could become as gods.

By knowing the law the Jews also learned how to break the law, and in breaking the law they discovered the incredible and improbable concept of Sin which gave them the key to unlock the mystery of their own humanity. No longer could they blame all the disasters of life on the whims of arbitrary gods, for human tragedy did not come from trying to compete with gods more powerful than themselves, nor from making mistakes, nor from breaking taboos, but from living a disorderly life in an orderly world. The Jew could choose to be an enemy of God, but by doing so he only ended up becoming his own worst enemy. Or he could obey God and be at one with the world around him. The choice was his. By following God's orders he could maintain order in his own life and enjoy something of that inner peace we are all looking for, that "shalom" which the Jew found in the tranquillity of order.

By obeying God's laws the Jews discovered that they had a place to stand above the quicksand of pagan doubt and despair. They could stand back and look more objectively at all the mysterious and terrifying forces playing havoc with their lives, and in doing so they found that these mysterious forces were not as terrifying as they had originally seemed. By worshipping the Master of the Universe the universe itself paled into relative insignificance and the shackles of religious devotion fell away from all created things. Before the God of the Jews the river gods fled, the sky gods retreated into the heavens, every other god turned to dust, and Mother Nature became truly natural for the first time. At long last, because men focused their devotion elsewhere, the heavens and the earth were free to be themselves rather than a pantheon of supernatural gods vying for our allegiance. Now the Jews, and those who followed in their footsteps, could begin to appreciate women as equal human beings because they no longer had to treat them as goddesses, and they could use material things for their own enjoyment because they no longer had to worship them as idols.

I found that when I began to look at the world through the eyes of a Jew it was rather like looking through the wrong end of a telescope. The powers that once governed my life become clearer and more distinct than ever before, but smaller and less significant. Because people and things, though they all reflected something of God's glory, were no longer gods, I was able to appreciate them for their real worth without having to make demands on them that they could not possibly fulfil. I could adore my wife as she is because I did not have to place her on some sort of divine pedestal. Even my children could be cherished, trained and protected as real human beings once I stopped making the foolish mistake of calling them little angels. In spite of spending most of my time changing their nappies and seeing that they did not swallow the bottle of aspirins nor step on the dog's tail, I knew that even as babies they were actually made in the image of God and capable of becoming complete persons just as God is completely personal. I even prayed that someday they might become like God, but only because I did not dare treat them as though they themselves were gods.

If I had been born an old fashioned Jew I would have honoured my children for what they might become, insisting with the psalmist that God had created them a little lower than the angels to crown them with glory and honour. Unlike the pagans about me I would not have placed them on the burning pyres of human sacrifice. Neither would I have thrown those I did not want over the cliffs into the sea in the manner of the ancient Greeks. Nor would I have sent them floating down the sewers of ancient Rome. For that matter I do not think that I would have had them aborted as we do in modern England, no matter how awkward or inconvenient their births might be.

As I could love my children for what they might become, I could honour my parents for showing me something of what God is like. I could begin to appreciate my father as a faint image of God once I came to accept God as my real Father. By calling God "Father" I was not blaming Him for squandering all the shopping money on drink nor accusing Him of beating up my mother every night he came home from the pub. In spite of my natural father's sins, I was simply recognizing that his wisdom and justice and mercy, to say nothing of the fact that he brought me into this world in the first place, all fit in with what I had come to know about God Himself. I came to realize that when I call God Father, I am not really saying much about God at all, but I am saying a great deal about what human fathers can be like.

I have come to discover what people and things are really like, apart from how they may first appear, in much the same sort of way that scientists first discovered helium. With the aid of a spectroscope they originally found this mysterious element in the sun, and then, believing that the earth came from the sun, they looked for it closer to home, eventually finding it lurking in the caves and dens of the earth. In much the same sort of way I have found unexpected signs of the wonder and glory of God lurking in the deep recesses of the souls of my five children. It would never have occurred to me however to look for these intimations of divine glory in such unlikely places, if I had not already seen something of the wonder and glory of God Himself. And if this is the case with my own children, how much more of my neighbours, to say nothing of my enemies or even of myself.

Though I was not born a Jew, I have discovered that all these Jewish attitudes have always been part of my own mental furniture. In spite of being a gentile, my culture has given me a Jewish way of looking at things. Moreover, upon examination, I find that these attitudes and the beliefs on which they were originally built all make sense to me. They fit my experience and satisfy a deep yearning within me. They liberate me from slavery to my own passions and give direction and purpose to my life. By consciously accepting the faith of the Jews I discover a new sense of inner peace with the world and everyone in it, no matter what personal trials and tragedies may come my way.

This does not mean that I am inevitably tied to these beliefs. Just as the Jew can always reject His God, so I can reject the God of the Jews if I so wish, and choose instead to be an atheist. In fact, come to think of it, it is only because I have been brought up with a Jewish cast of mind that I am free to be an atheist. I can deny the reality of God only because I have been taught to believe in the kind of God who can be denied. I find that pagans do not doubt the existence of the gods because they do not think about the gods. They experience them and there is no way anyone can consciously deny his own experience. But the Jew has been told about God, and everyone is free to disbelieve what he is told. Only Jews, and those of us who have adopted the faith of the Jews, are free to deny the faith.

Any of us may decide not to believe in God, but it is only the God of the Jews that we decide not to believe in, for all of us are children of Abraham if only by adoption. We think in no other terms and know of no other gods. We are not able to worship new gods of our own making no matter how much we try because we always know that they are of our own making. Nor are we free to worship the gods of the ancient pagans for we buried them long ago. Much like a woman who divorces her husband, we may reject the Jewish God of our forefathers but we can never again regain our pagan virginity.

From time to time small groups of people, like those who gather every year at Stonehenge to perform their Rites of Spring, try to resurrect the old pagan gods. But they can never bring it off for the simple reason that whereas ancient druids were natural pagans who never tried to be anything other than themselves, these modern druids are only dissatisfied secularists desperately trying to be something other than themselves. They fail to realize that none of us can deny our cultural inheritance, even if we deny the faith upon which that inheritance has been built. After four thousand years our culture has been permeated through and through with the Jewish understanding of God, so that now only two choices are open to us. Either we believe in the God of the Jews or else we become out-and-out secularists who believe in nothing at all, not even in ourselves.

If I have to choose, I know that I would much rather believe in the God of the Jews than believe in nothing at all, but what right do I have to make such a choice? Just because I have been raised to think that there is a just and loving God who cares for me, does not mean that my thinking is correct. I must have some evidence before I can believe in the God of the Jews, and here I find that the Jews themselves are of very little help.

The ancient Jews were never much good at defending their beliefs either by logical argument or scientific experiment, nor did they produce a single first rate philosopher until comparatively late in their history. Though I suppose their approach to life could be called scientific in the sense that they were among the first people ever to respect the laws of cause and effect, yet when it came to their belief in God they were about as unscientific as we can imagine. In defending their belief they simply insisted that God had personally revealed Himself to them in ways they could not possibly prove either by scientific experiment or by any other kind of earthly evidence. If you were to ask an Old Testament Jew how he knew about God, all he could have said is that God Himself had told him. "Thus says the Lord" is his constant refrain.

For all I know the belief that they had received some sort of personal revelation from God may have satisfied these ancient Jews, but it is not of much help to me today. I am not going to stake my life on a faith I have learned about only from hearsay, even if the Jews claim that it is divine hearsay. Such blind faith offends the modern mind and flies in the face of all my training. Just as I would rebel against anyone who tried to make me accept what they say simply because they say it or believe what they believe just because they believe it, so I turn a deaf ear to anyone who asks me to accept what God says simply because some ancient people once claimed that He said it. Just as Scrooge thought the ghost of Marley may have been nothing more than a bit of undigested beef, so for all I know the Word of the Lord may have been nothing more than a pathological ringing in the Jewish ear.

On the other hand, if God really is personal it is very hard to see how we could possibly believe in Him unless he did reveal Himself to us in some kind of personal way. I certainly do not place my faith in my friends through some kind of scientific analysis or philosophical speculation. I know them through their autobiographies, and my faith in them depends upon what they choose to reveal about themselves. Whether written or not, the story of their lives gives me my only authentic insight into their real character and personality.

I suppose that someone could point to all sorts of evidence that my wife is a thief and a liar. Yet I ignore what they say because I know from living with her over a period of years that she is not that sort of a person. I have faith in her because I have chosen to believe in her, but this is not an arbitrary choice nor some kind of wishful thinking on my part. It is based on a close and intimate relationship which has taught me that she can be trusted in spite of any evidence to the contrary. She has revealed herself to me, and if others wonder what she is really like, they must either take my word for it or else come to know her as I do.

I find that I am constantly placing this same kind of faith in all sorts of other people, even though there is no clear scientific evidence for doing so. The cynic, if he so wishes, can quite easily demonstrate that several people are out to kill me. He may point out that some of my closest friends talk behind my back and that others keep poison in the garden shed. Just yesterday a friend asked me to climb a ladder from which I could easily have fallen and broken my neck. Yet in spite of all the evidence I do not go about fearing for my life. I am saved from being paranoid because I realize that most people do not know me well enough to care whether I am dead or alive, and those few who do know me well enough seem quite content to let me go on living. I cannot prove scientifically that they are not out to kill me, and indeed I can think of all sorts of reasons why they might, but the better I come to know them the harder it is to think that murder is really on their minds.

I cannot say as much for trees and stones. From what I can tell stones are extremely callous about my welfare, and as for trees, the only reason it never occurs to me that murder might be on their minds is that they seem so remarkably mindless. The law of averages assures me that most trees are not going to fall in my path and strike me dead, though I still walk somewhat warily through the woods knowing that at any moment one of them might accidentally do so. But if in the woods I meet a friend, we walk together with complete confidence in one another, because, for some strange reason beyond my comprehension, I know that my friends do not wish my immediate demise. Though I do not deserve it, they really do seem to care for me. In fact, it is precisely because there is no earthly reason why they have to care for me, that my friends, unlike stones and trees, reveal themselves as free and caring people with minds and wills of their own.

So the Jews thought it was with God. They did not suffer from pagan paranoia because they did not think that God was out to get them, even though they often thought they deserved it. Neither was God callous like a stone nor mindless like trees. Instead, God had revealed Himself as a caring sort of person who, throughout their history had never betrayed them even though they had often betrayed Him. In their history God had remained faithful, and by doing so He had given the Jews their faith. This is a personal faith, but one which we can share either by accepting the Jew's word for what he says about God or else by coming to know God in the same way the Jew today comes to know Him.

The modern Jew does not come to know God through some kind of philosophical or theological speculation but from hearing the stories of his ancestors. Going to the synagogue every Friday evening, the young Jewish child hears from his father's bank manager or perhaps from the neighbourhood grocer the stories of Abraham, the Father of his own nation, and of Moses, the mediator between God and man, whom God called to bring freedom to the Jewish slaves in Egypt. These stories give him his national inheritance and make him think like a Jew whether consciously or not. In much the same sort of way I became an American and learned American ideals and values by hearing stories about George Washington, the Father of my Country who never told a lie, and about Abraham Lincoln, the mediator who brought freedom to the American slaves. Yet there is a difference between the two. In all the American stories the local heroes are always the chief actors, but in the Jewish stories the chief actor is God Himself who by acting in the life of His people reveals what He is like and what He likes. Divine revelation is God's autobiography written into the pages of Jewish history.

It was not long before I came to realize that what was true of the modern Jew was to some extent also true of me. I was also raised in a kind of synagogue, only it was called Sunday School and Church. And there, by hearing the stories of Abraham and Moses, I too gradually came to think somewhat like a Jew. Those slaves in Egypt were my own ancestors, and in freeing them from tyranny God had made it crystal clear just what He wanted the world to be like. I took it for granted that He had established certain laws for running the world, and, come what may, just so long as I obeyed these laws everything would be alright. Without thinking much about it, I rather assumed that in the end the righteous will always win the day by always doing what is right. As a kind of spiritual Jew I believed that every story should have a happy ending and that, if I was a good little boy and did what I was told, I too would live happily ever after and not be thrown on the rubbish heap of the world's disasters.

Like just about everyone else in our culture I came to take most all of this for granted without thinking much about it. I unwittingly accepted the Jewish faith with neither argument nor proof. And yet this was not that blind faith once described by the American humorist, Mark Twain, as "believing what you know ain't so". Far from it. Just as my faith in my wife's honesty is based upon my personal experience of her, so I came to discover that the personal faith I had inherited from the Jews could also be tested by personal experience.

Logic seems to demand that if anything exists some sort of god or gods must exist, but only I can decide to put my faith in a personal God who is supposed to care for me. Ultimately the faith of the Jew is a moral choice which only I can make. No-one can make it for me any more than someone else can convince me that I ought to trust my wife. The most anyone can do is point the way, retell the age old story and invite me to "taste and see that the Lord is good".

Believe It or Not

A crocodile sheds its crocodile tears

5

Pain and Grief

It is no use at all telling me to "taste and see that the Lord is good" when I am standing at the side of a hospital bed watching someone's son dying of cancer. Instead I taste nothing but bitterness and feel only anger and indescribable pain. In his parent's eyes I see frustration, helplessness and a sense of terrible injustice. "Why", they beg, "does God take our son when he never did anything wrong in his life?" And of course they are right. Life is terribly unfair, and it does no good pretending otherwise. If God is to have an important place in my life I shall first demand that He answers the searchings of their broken hearts.

For that matter what answer does He have for my own heart-aches? The people closest to me are suddenly wrenched away and something of my own self dies within me. I continue to go about my business as best I can, but inside I feel only half the person I once was, and wonder how much more can be taken from me before there is nothing left of me at all. I look to other people for support, but find that most of them do not want to know. Even those I thought were my closest friends suddenly turn and stab me in the back, and in my own family, where I might expect the kind of care I so desperately need, everyone seems much too busy with their own affairs to pay much attention to me.

It would seem that there is neither justice nor faithfulness in a world where no-one really cares about anyone except themselves.

If, in desperation, I turn to God, He pays me back by letting my son die of cancer. And I find that He fares little better on the stage of world history where I find the twisted bodies of six million of His chosen people massacred in the Nazi gas chambers. Nor does the situation improve when I turn to the Christian Church, for there, instead of seeing a community of love, I discover a holy club of fighting factions each proclaiming its own self righteousness. Abandoning all hope of finding supernatural love, I look for signs of purely natural affection, only to find thousands of children sexually molested and physically tortured by their parents.

This may be too depressing for those who spend their days whistling in the darkness of the world's disasters, but in my search for God I believe that I must try to see things as they really are. When I do, signs of God's goodness are anything but clear. There is such a depressing amount of pain and grief about me that I sometimes wonder if depression should be treated as a sign of health rather than disease, and that our only real martyrs are those who have the courage to destroy themselves. Perhaps the world's suicides are the only ones who really know what life is all about.

It all depends of course on what it is that makes us so depressed. I find, for instance, that poverty does not seem to depress the poor until they have some idea of what money could buy if only they were rich. There was even a time when people seemed to manage quite well without television, but now one of the most traumatic things that can happen is to have the television set break down during the Christmas holidays when all the children are at home. I even find that I do not actually get depressed when my enemy stabs me in the back, no matter how painful the stabbing may be, unless he turns out to be someone I had always thought of as my friend. Suffering may actually goad me into action and I can accept death itself unless it takes me completely by surprise.

It would seem that it is not pain and grief in themselves that depress us, but disappointed expectations. When I am disappointed or let down, or suddenly deprived of my rights, or come up against injustice where I expected just the opposite, I then begin to sense that something terribly evil is happening to me.

If I believed that my sense of justice only existed in my own heart, or that hope is nothing more than a cruel joke of the gods written into my own psyche, then I would have no problem with evil nor with my faith in God. Pain and grief never seemed to make the ancient pagans doubt their faith in the gods because they never believed in the goodness of the gods in the first place. Nor did it ever occur to them, any more than it occurs to the modern cynic, that the forces governing the universe were either good or evil. They were just very inconvenient, so that, in the face of cosmic cruelty, the only sane philosophy was to eat, drink and be merry for tomorrow everyone would die. In the meantime pain and grief were to be avoided as much as possible, and when death came endurance rather than faith was the only virtue really worth having.

Unlike the ancient pagan or modern cynic, I find that I keep asking what kind of justice allows innocent babies to be tortured. For some strange reason I cannot rid my mind of the belief that somewhere or other there must be some kind of real justice. I feel it in my bones and believe it in my heart, and when things go wrong this sense of justice keeps me awake at night and wears me down throughout the day. I have been taught to place my faith in a God who cares for his people, and every time a child dies that faith comes under attack in much the same sort of way that any suggestion that my wife has lied tempts me to doubt her honesty. I only worry about the world's suffering and the possibility that my wife has lied because I believe that my wife is basically honest and that justice can be found on the earth. I am only horrified by evil because I have come to place my faith in divine goodness.

Gangs of criminals do not go around worrying about the problem of crime, nor do drug addicts worry about the drug problem. Crime for them is normal and drugs a way of life. If, however, they are converted from their life of crime or try to overcome their drug addiction, then the existence of drugs and crime becomes a real problem for the first time and as likely as not they will talk about little else. They go on crusades to fight against crime. They devote their lives to rehabilitating other drug addicts. They organise campaigns to wipe out these evils from our social life. Having come to believe that it is good to live in an honest society of clear headed people, they do everything they can to stamp out whatever evil tries to destroy it.

Being neither a converted criminal nor a former drug addict, I perhaps lack some of their zeal in trying to rid the world of evil. But though I make no great claims for the strength of my own conscience, I am sure that if I had the means I also would do my best to wipe out crime and drug addiction. And if I were God I would never let earthquakes destroy whole villages nor allow the Nazis to gas six million Jews. I would rid the world of debilitating diseases, children's deformities and every other kind of agony that afflicts the human race. Yet God, who supposedly can do something about all these evils, apparently cannot be bothered. It would seem that He is not as good as converted gangs of criminals nor as trustworthy as my wife, unless, of course, He is no more able to rid the world of evil than I am. How then, I wonder, can I possibly be asked to believe in a God who either has no conscience or who is too weak to obey what conscience He has?

Perhaps the old fashioned atheist was right after all, for he at least let God off the hook by denying that He even existed. Instead of placing all the world's evils on God's shoulders, perhaps I would do better to think that my deep seated belief in justice really is nothing more than a figment of a corporate imagination created out of our psychological need to be treated fairly.

There seems to be no easy answer. My sense of evil comes from a conviction that there must be some kind of real and objective justice not of my own making, and that pain and grief are evil because they go against divine goodness. Yet my very sense of evil makes me doubt the divine goodness from whence it comes. I become acutely aware of a devastating contradiction, built into the very fabric of the universe, which I find almost impossible to resolve. If there is no God who looks after me out of the goodness of His heart, then what I tend to call evil is really nothing more than personal unpleasantness. If there is such a God reigning supreme over our lives, then all the evil in the world goes against everything I have come to believe about Him.

It did not take long to discover that I was not the only person who had ever noticed this apparent contradiction between evil and divine goodness. Throughout the centuries people have been trying to come up with some kind of satisfactory solution, though I have found that most of their solutions never really seemed to solve anything. The ancient Jews themselves wrote about the problem of evil in the book of Job, but the only answer they came to was that God was far too mysterious and much too powerful for us to question what He does. They may have been right, but I must say that I do not find it very easy to place my trust in a God I am not allowed to question. Others have claimed that we are all so evil that we only get what we deserve, and that, far from complaining about our pain and grief, we ought to thank God that life isn't even worse than it is. I found this impossible to accept, for though I may deserve everything that comes my way, I cannot believe an innocent child deserves to be tortured by his parents or that the Jews were more wicked than their German persecutors. Many would agree with me but still argue that even if life is not very fair we will all get our just rewards in heaven. And for all I know they also may be right, but it does not explain why God made life on earth so very unfair in the first place.

Finding no help from these common attempts to explain the world's evil, I turned to professional theologians, and in their weighty tomes read about all sorts of subtle distinctions invented to solve the problem. They talked about such things as God's "active will" and His "permissive will", claiming that God does not want little children tortured, but in order to bring about some greater good He allows it to happen. I found this quite beyond belief to say nothing of being extremely distasteful, for what, I asked, could possibly be good enough to excuse the torture of little children?

None of these attempts to explain away the problem of evil made any sense to me until I actually tasted pain and grief myself. And now, though I still cannot fully grasp why there is so much suffering in the world, my own pain has at least given me a glimpse into how this suffering can be part of the mystery of God's goodness rather than something which goes against it.

First I discovered that there is a surprising difference between my own personal suffering and the atrocities I read about in the daily newspapers, for even though these atrocities are almost always much worse than anything I have ever experienced myself, they rarely, if ever, make me question my faith. It is only when something terrible happens to me that my faith is likely to be shattered.

I find that the same thing is true even when tragedy comes to my closest friends. There is only the difference of one letter between a telegram that says "Our son is dead" and one that says "Your son is dead", but this small difference makes all the difference in the world. Originally I would have thought that the first telegram might shatter my faith in a God who could do such a terrible thing to my friends, and the second possibly threaten what little faith I have in myself by raising doubts about my genuine feelings towards my son. I find, however, that it almost always works the other way round. I begin to question my feelings towards my friends when tragedy strikes, but only question my faith in God when something terrible happens directly to me. It is as though the only real evil in the world is the evil that I feel in myself. And of course in a sense this is true, for it is only when I suffer personally that suffering suddenly seems really evil.

This is not to deny that I am horrified at other people's suffering but only that the horror I feel requires an effort of imagination on my part. such that their suffering becomes my suffering as well. I can watch a James Bond film in which people are stabbed or poisoned or blown up out of island fortresses and never feel the least twinge of pain or grief about their fate. Let the same thing happen to real people and I may not be able to watch the film because I begin to feel something of their own suffering in myself. Through my imagination some sort of mysterious exchange of pain takes place between myself and others which can easily become too great for me to bear.

This difference between real and imaginary pain can easily be blurred, making it extremely difficult for our imaginations to distinguish between the atrocities pictured on the 10 o'clock television news and those we see in a James Bond film. We must not blame television for this however, for all of us have built in defences which protect us from feeling both the real and imaginary sufferings of other people. I may be in a roomful of people when someone comes in and steps on everyone's toes. But even though the same thing happens to all of us, only my toes feel the pain. It takes a giant step of the imagination to realise that everyone else's toes hurt as much as mine. Some kind of protective barrier seems to be built into my psyche which protects me from all the pain surrounding me and makes me less sensitive towards other people's suffering.

This insensitivity acts as a kind of vaccine keeping me from being infected by other people's pain, and by helping me bear my own suffering it seems, on the face of it, to be a very healthy thing. Oddly enough, however, most people do not seem to see it this way. Instead they act as though there is something terribly wrong if I am insensitive towards the sufferings of others. Even at the risk of destroying my own peace of mind, they seem to think that I ought to take that giant step of the imagination which I need if I am going to grieve over other people's agony and feel their pain in my own heart.

I must confess that I rather think the same way myself even though it goes against the way I usually respond to misfortunes which do not affect me personally. I was recently watching a televised memorial service for people who had drowned when their pleasure boat sank in the River Thames, and though I felt sympathy for the mourners I realized that I was not feeling what they obviously felt. My heart went out to them, but it did not break. The odd thing is that I felt it would have been a good thing if my heart could have actually broken along with theirs, and I find that most people seem to agree with me. Few people, if any, blame Mother Theresa for identifying with the sufferings of the poor of Calcutta, but instead seem to think that her extreme expressions of loving care are something we should all try to cultivate in our own hearts. If my heart had broken along with those mourners on television, most people would praise me for my sympathetic understanding, no matter how much it would add to the weight of my personal pain and grief.

Here I find a strange paradox. People seem to think that I ought to take the sufferings of other people on my own shoulders, and yet they expect me to avoid at all costs any suffering that happens directly to me. If I feel the pain that others feel I am a saint, but if I inflict pain upon myself I am a masochist. Yet even then people will often praise me for certain kinds of suffering that I bring upon myself. If I choose to suffer for my country, to lay down my life for a friend or to die a martyr in the cause of justice, I will as likely as not be treated as some kind of hero and my actions held up as good and saintly examples for others to imitate as best they may. It would seem that far from being evil in themselves pain and grief are often seen as signs of goodness or even holiness.

I find that we are willing to accept and even embrace an incredible amount of suffering so long as it has some meaning or purpose either for ourselves or for others, and that it only seems evil when it appears to be pointless. And, in order to make some kind of sense out of this pointless suffering, we try to find someone who is responsible for it. Someone has to take the blame, and if we cannot blame someone we know, we are inclined to pin all the blame on a God we do not know.

It really seems rather foolish, however, to blame God for all the pointless pain and grief in the world when we almost never give Him credit for any of the good things that happen. If Ethiopians are starving we blame God for the drought, but if they are rescued from starvation we thank Christian Aid or Oxfam or a sudden change in the weather. This hardly seems fair, as understandable as it may be. I sometimes wonder what would happen if, instead of making God responsible for all the evil in the world, we treated Him as though He was one of its victims who needs our sympathy rather than blame. But then of course it would be rather difficult to know how to worship or even respect such a suffering God. By attempting to acquit Him of any blame for all the pain and grief in the world it would appear that I would have taken away His godhead.

I found all this quite beyond me until I suddenly realized that we would not be talking about the problem of evil at all if it were not for creatures like myself who are capable of suffering pain and grief in the first place. No-one questions the power or the goodness of God because level fields suddenly erupt into mountains or earthquakes hurl mountains into the sea. We do not mourn the death of mountains nor blame God for the destruction of fertile fields, but only doubt his goodness when people are living on the side of the mountains or ploughing the fields when they erupt. So long as all the violent cataclysms of the universe form one harmonious whole we can accept that God knows what He is doing and even marvel at the balance of nature demonstrated by these potentially catastrophic cataclysms. We only question God's goodness when human suffering follows in their wake.

Death and destruction in themselves do not make us doubt God's goodness, but only the personal suffering that so often goes along with them. The problem of evil is really the problem of our own sensitivity and self-consciousness, so that when I ask about all the evil in the world I am really asking about myself and my own feelings. I need to know why I feel so empty when my friends reject me and why something dies within me when my son dies of cancer. Why do I feel so distressed and even guilty when I see the distended bellies of starving Ethiopian children, or feel disgust and anger at the massacre of three million Cambodians in the "Killing Fields"? If I am going to blame God for all this evil, I will have to start by blaming Him for making me the kind of creature who is able to suffer so much pain and grief. What is it about me that God finds so precious that He will not give it up even though it brings so much anguish into my life?

Whatever it is that upsets me about starving Ethiopians and devastates me if my son dies of cancer, seems to most people, including myself, to be a good and holy thing. I thank God for whatever it is about me that makes it possible for me to feel pain and grief, for without it something very precious about my personality and character would be lost forever. As long as I can suffer I know that I have some kind of share in God's own loving goodness.

This is not to say, of course, that suffering is something good in itself. People who think like that have serious psychological problems and can be a real danger both to themselves and to other people. And if God thinks like that, He must be a real danger to His own creation. Far from liking suffering, God must surely find it much more offensive than any of us could possibly imagine, but apparently He is not able to get rid of it, even if it involves the torture of little children, without destroying something of His own goodness.

There are certain things that God simply cannot do. He cannot, for example, make a square circle because the idea of a square circle is nonsense and there is no nonsense with God. Nor can He fill a jug with water and leave it empty at the same time, so that even though He may decide to turn water into wine He cannot do it without getting rid of the water. There are actually some things God cannot do that I can do. He cannot tell lies or torture little children because that would go against His own goodness, but I can do both if I choose because I am not necessarily all that good. In other words even God cannot have His cake and eat it too. Unlike me, He cannot do silly or devilish things and still remain Himself. And if it should turn out that pain and grief reflect something of God's goodness, then this may possibly explain why He cannot get rid of it and still remain true to Himself.

How can I possibly think that my own personal suffering reflects something of God's own character? Or, to look at it the other way round, is there any way in which God actually suffers along with me? If He does, then perhaps we have stumbled upon the secret solution to the so-called problem of evil, for instead of being evil in itself, my suffering turns out to be an essential way in which I become like God, and should this be so, then it is no wonder that people treat martyrs as saints and think it is a good and holy thing to suffer for the sake of others. Though others suffer pain the anguish which I feel for their suffering comes from something God-like within me that distinguishes me from everything else that God has made.

Electrons do not cry out in anguish when they collide with other electrons, nor do stones mourn the loss of other stones as they watch them passing into the dust of the earth. Crocodiles never grieve the death of their victims when they shed their crocodile tears. But when I collide with my fellow men we both suffer for it, and I grieve when my friends return to the dust of the earth. I weep with those who weep and mourn with those who mourn, and these very tears make me more than just a cog in the wheel of fortune or an insignificant bundle of energy in a meaningless universe. If I were not aware of my own anguish and knew nothing of other people's tragedies, I would not know the evil of suffering, but I also would know nothing of caring for others nor ever share their loves and joys. Along with life and birth I would endure death and utter devastation, but I would be equally indifferent to both, feeling neither joy nor grief, neither gain nor loss.

If it were not for my ability to suffer I would be nothing more than a plaything in some kind of divine playground, indifferent to my own fate and to the fate of all the other toys. I could not be affected by the tragedies that come my way because I would be devoid of every kind of personal feeling and affection, and this, it seems to me, would be the worst evil of all, for it would destroy my personality and make me nothing more than an object created to satisfy the whimsical pleasures of arbitrary gods.

Instead of believing that I am made in the image of all those pagan gods who care nothing for my welfare, I have come to believe in a God who cares for me so much that He allows me to care along with Him, and I find that my capacity to suffer comes from this ability to care. I only grieve the loss of my leg because I care about walking, and I only mourn the loss of my friends because I love them. It is precisely this that sets me apart from the dog who bites my leg or the cancer that riddles the bodies of my friends. I am personal because I care, and because I care I also suffer.

In thinking about such things, I have gradually come to see that the problem of suffering is actually the problem of love, and if this is true of me it must in some sort of infinite way also be true of God. I suffer because I reflect in myself something of a God who loves me, and in some small way my own acts of love reflect His infinite love. It is a love which, like every kind of love, never follows the rules of logic. The heart does not have its reasons, contrary to what is sometimes said. Or rather it has no reasoning beyond itself. I have no idea why God gave me the power to reflect something of His own love, just as I do not know why He loves me in the first place. Even my closest friends are quick to point out that I am not very lovable, and yet I know God loves me because if He did not, He would never have made me in the first place. He can certainly get along perfectly well without me. But I am rather glad that He did make me, even with all the pain and grief that goes along with it.

If my pain and grief come from love, I do not see how they can be evil in themselves. In a mysterious sort of way they must be an essential part of love's goodness. And if God is infinite love it would seem to follow that He must have an infinite capacity for pain and grief. At the very least He must suffer when anything goes wrong with His creation, just as I suffer when something goes wrong with anything I have done. Yet God cannot suffer physically because He does not have a body, and His heart cannot actually break because He does not have a physical heart. Nor can He suffer from some sort of personal loss because God cannot lose anything.

As God neither suffers from any selfishness within Himself nor from anything inflicted upon Him from outside, it might be better not to use the word "suffering" at all when talking about Him. A much better word would be "self-sacrifice". Only by learning the meaning of sacrificial love will we come to terms with our own pain and grief and find the key for solving the problem of evil. We must find out what it means to say, not only that God loves us, but that God Himself is Love.

BELIEVE IT OR NOT

The Supreme Sacrifice

6

All You Need Is Love

If only the poor benighted lamb was able to understand the true significance of sacrificial love, he would rejoice at the honour I bestow upon him as he is led to the slaughterhouse in preparation for my Sunday dinner. With the same knowledge even the unfeeling cabbage, as it is thrown into the stewing pot, might appreciate that it is fulfilling a fundamental law of exchange governing the entire universe. By such noble and sacrificial acts the woolly sheep and leafy cabbage are miraculously transformed into becoming a part of something as marvellous as me.

So it is at every level of life. As the insignificant minnow is sucked into the maw of the awesome whale should it not rejoice that it has contributed to the whale's might? Were not the ancients right in killing the kingly lion not just for food but for its skin, which, when worn in solemn ceremony, might bestow upon the killer something of the lion's strength? I sometimes ask myself if it is it too much to hope that in some unknown heavenly realm the potential chicken is thankful that it has sustained me by never progressing beyond the docile egg I consume for breakfast, or that the very rocks and vegetation, lying lifeless upon the autumn ground, are singing out their silent praises to whatever god made it possible for them, by their unstinting act of quiet sacrifice, to be transformed into the soil in which I plant the cabbages that give me life. It would seem that even in the autumn leaves there are signs of a universal law of sacrifice transforming everything into a future glory beyond its wildest dreams.

Just as cabbage heads and kingly lions are transformed into the glory of our humanity, so by our own personal sacrifices we are caught up into the realms inhabited by the gods. Imagine the thrill of being chosen as this year's annual human sacrifice. Lying upon the burning pyre or standing above the yawning chasm waiting to be thrown to the expectant gods, you would know that you were the very best your tribe could offer, and that in some mysterious sort of way you were making it possible for your family and all your friends to fulfil their own eternal destiny. For a moment fear of the unknown might have held you back from the brink of certain death, but then all hesitation would have been overwhelmed by the same rush of exaltation and excitement a young man or woman might feel today if chosen to represent their country in the Olympic Games.

There was, however, one small but serious flaw in all these ancient practices. Sacrificial offerings require sacrificial victims and the victims always end up the worse for wear. Unlike the Olympic Games where participants usually have some hope of winning, sacrificial victims lying upon burning pyres or falling into yawning chasms always appear the losers. What is true of men and women is also true of sheep and cabbages and every other kind of sacrificial victim, so that even though I may become healthier by consuming my breakfast egg, I hardly do the potential chicken any good. It is difficult to see how there can be any justice in a law of universal sacrifice which can only give us strength and glory by victimizing creatures weaker than ourselves or create new life by preying upon the deaths of others.

We can attempt, of course, to by-pass this universal law of sacrifice or at least minimize some of its worst effects. We have now given up throwing people over cliffs or burning them alive on funeral pyres, and I suppose I could reduce the massacre of unborn chickens and ease the hurt of slaughterhouse sheep by becoming a vegetarian. But even then, if I am to save my own life, I would still have to slaughter the insentient cabbage. By refusing to sacrifice the lamb in the slaughterhouse of human gluttony, I do not save its life. Instead I only allow it to die a natural death where it ends up fertilizing the ground from which the insentient cabbage grows. Even for the vegetarian it seems there can be no life without some form of sacrificial death.

I know that if I sacrifice myself to either gods or men my only sure reward is death, and that by giving my life away I only lose what little life I have. Should I be re-incarnated after my untimely death into some other form of earthly life, as some people like to think, it still would do me no good, for what I might become would have no connection with what I once had been. By becoming something other than myself, no matter what, I would lose the only life and personality, character and humanity that I have ever had.

I not only loose my life by giving it away. I cannot even give away my prize possessions and still keep them for myself. When Suzie asks to have a bite of Joey's chocolate bar, he quite sensibly refuses to give her any if he wants all of it for himself, and though we may scold him for being selfish, we certainly cannot condemn him for being stupid. Yet there are some things Joey can give away and still keep for himself, or may even end up having more as a result. If he is watching a television show and refuses to let Suzie into the room because he wants to watch all of the show himself, or will not tell Suzie about a story he is reading because he wants to know the entire story, we are not so likely to criticize him for being selfish as to laugh at him for being so incredibly foolish. He ought to realize that he will not know any less of the story by telling Suzie what he knows, nor will he lose some of the television programme by sharing it with others.

Of course, real children are quite aware of this. If Joey tries to keep Suzie out of the television room, it is not because he wants to keep all the television show for himself, but because he is afraid that, by talking all the time or by finding other ways to draw attention to herself, she may ruin the show for both of them.

In such childish bickering I found an important clue to the secret of my own personality. For Joey and Suzie taught me that although physical things like rocks and chocolate bars are lost by being shared, many other things, such as knowledge and pleasure and love, need to be shared in order to be fully appreciated and enjoyed. Sharing what I know, and the pleasures I enjoy, actually clarifies my knowledge and makes my enjoyment more intense. Even though I cannot have my cake and eat it too, or give away a chocolate bar and keep it for myself, I can enjoy the cake and chocolate all the more when others enjoy them with me.

All good teachers know that the best way to learn is to teach, and in similar fashion I find that I usually enjoy a Rembrandt painting or Beethoven symphony much more when I am enjoying them with someone else. More dramatically, I find that when I am caught up in the enthusiasm of a large crowd of like-minded people, as at some great rock concert or political rally, I feel my mind gradually transformed by the general mood of the crowd. I discover, as I am carried away by the general enthusiasm, feelings of love or hatred in myself I never knew before. By losing my individuality in the crowd I discover a new life for the first time. I die to myself and suddenly I am alive.

The greatest mystery in my life is the undeniable fact that when I am not thinking about myself I begin to find myself for the first time. If I get involved in helping old age pensioners or in protecting the rights of little children, I contribute something towards their welfare, but if I start wondering if I really have anything to contribute, I begin to spend most of my energy thinking about myself and give up helping others altogether. If I am at a party and get so caught up in the conversation that I completely forget myself, I am likely to realize after I get home that I was really quite clever at the time. If, however, I start wondering at the party if I am being very clever, I will probably turn shy and be quite incapable of saying anything at all. In the same sort of way a musician only gives a good performance when he is so absorbed in what he is doing that he does not have a chance to ask himself whether he is giving a good performance. He only makes mistakes when he starts thinking more about his ability to play the music than about the music he is playing.

In thinking about such things I began to see that personal sacrifice in itself is not necessarily destructive, but that certain things, like knowledge and love and pleasure, actually grow by being given away, and that by dying to self I actually begin to live a fuller life. Perhaps this is why I am profoundly moved by television films depicting soldiers sacrificing their lives to help mates escape from war time prison camps, and why my heart goes out in wonder and admiration to the Polish priest, Maximilian Kolbe, who, in exchange for the life of one of his parishioners, offered himself up to a slow and tortuous death in a Nazi prison camp. I understand why the Roman Catholic Church has made him a saint, and I hope that some day they may do the same for Mother Theresa. When I see her caring for the lifeless poor in the forgotten streets of Calcutta, I am stirred by an emotion far greater than mere admiration.

From her example and that of thousands of others, I know that there is a kind of love far different from the popular self-centred love which cries out to the beloved, "I desperately need you and cannot live without you". There is a sacrificial love as hard as life itself, a love that is willing to give everything to another without counting the cost and which I know I need to cultivate if I am to survive this life with any real peace of mind.

Yet I must confess that when I wonder if I too might be called upon to live the life of a Mother Theresa, or imitate the death of Maximilian Kolbe, fear holds me back from such total commitment as it once held back the human victims of ancient sacrificial rites. Though something within me makes me want to be like these modern martyrs, a much stronger force makes me want to preserve my own life and comfort even more.

The instinct for self preservation usually wins the day with me. Far from handing myself over to sacrificial love, I strengthen my defences and raise protective walls whenever I feel threatened by love's demands. Knowing that life is fragile and that pain and grief inexorably follow in the wake of personal sacrifice, I avoid getting very involved in other people's lives and learn instead to stand on my own two feet. In a desperate search for security, I shrink back in fear at any suggestion that I might actually find my real life by losing it, and defend myself by arguing that God helps those who help themselves, or, in a less religious vein, that if you do not look out for number one there is no-one else who will.

This self-centredness of mine may not be very admirable but at least it makes good sense. My only real problem is that I am not nearly as sensible as I would like to think, so that just as I am convinced that I should look after my own self interests and forget everyone else, the incomprehensible love of Maximilian Kolbe and Mother Theresa rises up to haunt me once again. Why, I wonder, can I never rest easy with the logic of my own selfishness? Why am I never praised for being so logical? Deep within me I find a never ending conflict between my own self-interest and the high expectations of sacrificial love such that I either feel guilty for being so selfish or else foolish for being so loving.

I only began to see my way out of this predicament when I came to realize that sacrificial love comes much more naturally to me than my own selfishness. I find that I only think about myself when there is something wrong with me. I only talk about my feet if I have sore feet and only think about my head when I have a headache, whereas I think about animals and children and friends whether there is anything wrong with them or not, and if they suffer I really do care about them even though their suffering may be none of my business. I think I really do believe in sacrificial love after all, and only put myself first when I feel under threat from the self-seeking interests of my family, friends or associates, or from an environment that seems to care nothing about me whatsoever.

I suspect that I believe in sacrificial love, no matter how illogical it may be, for the simple reason that it has made me what I am. I would never have been born if there had not been some sort of love between my natural parents, even should it have been nothing more than a pretence of "making love" at the time of my conception. Then after my birth, my very life depended upon an unending routine of parental sacrifice which I took completely for granted precisely because it came so naturally. Also, had it not been for my teachers at school I would now be little more than an imbecile, and were it not for the love of my friends I would be a psychological wreck.

From my own observation I have learned that there can be no real growth nor even life without some kind of sacrifice. But this still does little good for the victims who are sacrificed. The slaughtered lamb and boiled cabbage may come into their own by keeping me alive, but they still remain victims of a never ending struggle for survival which in the end they must always lose. Even the mother who sacrifices every personal pleasure to slave unceasingly for her children's welfare, as often as not ends up with little or nothing to show for all her efforts.

Yet I have also noticed that such self-sacrificing mothers bear little resemblance to all those other sacrificial victims who are led unwillingly or unknowingly to their untimely deaths. What makes all the difference is that a mother's daily acts of personal sacrifice are done willingly in love. From thinking about my own mother, and all the sacrifices she has made for me, I have come to see that her life of sacrifice is precisely what has given her her strength and creative energy. If it were not for her incomprehensible love for me all these same sacrifices would have merely victimized her.

We do not stand out as unique individuals by clinging to our meagre possessions, but by giving ourselves willingly to one another in such a way that, through habitual acts of personal sacrifice, a mysterious and explosive exchange of character, interests and personality takes place in the deepest recesses of our souls. And it seems to me that if this is true of us it must be preeminently true of the God who made us. If there is any kind of personal creator then some sort of sacrificial love on His part must have been the explosive force or "big bang" which created you and me in the first place. It really does look as though it is love that makes the world go round and that self-abandonment is the key to creativity, even though only human beings seem aware of the fact.

Ever since I was a child I have been told that God is love, but it never really seemed to make any difference to anyone until the Sixties generation came along. Then all of a sudden we were told that "all you need is Love". The gospel of love was shouted from the housetops by long haired hippies and screamed through amplifiers by rock musicians. A new faith taught the world that its problems would be resolved by love, and a new morality demanded that nations should make love, not war.

It all seemed terribly exciting at first, but then a cynical generation turned its back on youthful optimism and wrote off love as the unrealistic morality of a hopelessly romantic idealism. Yet the young prophets of the sixties did not fail because their message of love was unrealistic. They failed because they never became radical enough to fully grasp the meaning of their own message. The Hollywood films of the Thirties and Forties had made them, along with all the rest of us, far too sentimental to understand the real meaning of love and much too soft to put into action the love they proclaimed. Too idealistic ever to become true revolutionaries, reaction was bound to set in and aggression take the place of sentimentality. Punks succeeded hippies and substituted hate for love, knowing that life is neither a bed of roses nor a refuge for flower children. Instead of making love they blew their minds with drugs until even the drugs betrayed them and their hearts drowned in a torrent of self-pity and remorse.

The slogans of love went sour because they failed to point out that love is a two-edged sword which, though it may make the world go round, all too often makes the world go wrong. As well as being the source of life, love is also the cause of almost all our pain and grief, teaching us the bitterness of tears even as it holds out the hope of personal fulfilment and happiness.

We need to be loved and, under the surface of our lives, there remains a lurking fear that our need will remain unfulfilled and our love unreturned. The spiritual cancers of unrequited love are never far away, no matter how deeply we may bury them in the inner recesses of our hearts. We need a few people at least who are willing to sacrifice themselves for our sakes without any conditions or strings attached. We cry out to be caught up in that world of sacrificial love where men and women willingly lay down their lives for their friends. We need to feel that we are worth dying for, and to be worshipped and adored through physical acts of sacrificial love. We need someone to say to us, as the old Anglican Prayer Book so rightly had a man say to his new wife in the middle of the marriage service, "With my body I thee worship."

When that worship is withdrawn and love unreturned, we suddenly feel alienated and intolerably betrayed, and our original love all too easily slips into unremitting hate. We discover a terrible disorder at the heart of sacrificial love which breeds spiritual death as well as life, destruction as well as growth. To most people, living in a world strewn with the bodies of every kind of sacrificial victim from rejected parents to neglected children, every form of sacrifice seems to be the potential enemy of creativity and every death the denial of personal fulfilment.

And yet, in spite of all the fruitless pain of sacrificial victims and the anguish brought upon us by our need for love, I have also had to face the fact that almost all the Christians I have ever known, and apparently also the Jews who went before them, have insisted that we were placed on this earth to order the world according to God's law of sacrificial love, and that self-centredness creates a disorder so vast that eventually it is capable of turning the whole planet, and even the entire universe, from a Garden of Eden into a Vale of Tears. Selfishness, they insist, is sin no matter how logical it may appear, and, as St Paul put it, "The wages of sin is death" - death not only for ourselves but for the entire universe. At the heart of Christian morality I find a thorough-going condemnation of private greed which may go against the modern grain but appears to be vindicated daily now that the frightening planetary effect of our so-called enlightened self-interest is being so thoroughly demonstrated by the "Greens", just as its evil effects upon society were once denounced by the Socialists.

Even though all would agree that victimisation and death are always evil in themselves, I could not fail to notice that Christians also insist that the deaths of the martyrs are not a defeat but the very food of the church, and that being haunted by the sacrificial lives of Mother Theresa and Maximilian Kolbe is not an illusion but an intimation of future glory. I came to see that, for the believing Christian, the life and death of Jesus is not just a moving story about some sort of incomprehensible deal made between Himself and His father in order to keep us all out of Hell. It unleashes a power which is able to transform every human sacrifice from an instrument of victimization to a source of personal fulfilment. Either the death of Jesus occurred on a Friday that really was good - the best Friday that there has ever been - or else every personal sacrifice is a waste of human life and Mother Theresa is a benign but deluded fool.

At this point I knew that I had to make some sort of sense out sacrificial love or else reject it altogether. If Mother Theresa is a fool I can safely remain in my own self-centredness. If however she, along with Maximilian Kolbe and so many thousands of others, hold the key to my ultimate happiness and personal fulfilment then I must walk the road of sacrificial love no matter where it leads. I knew that there was no middle road and that none of us can stand at the crossroads forever, but I still did not know how to decide which road I ought to take.

It seemed obvious that if I were to follow the road of sacrificial love, I would have to see this love actually winning the day over hatred and selfishness. If in spite of all the evidence to the contrary, I was also to believe that God Himself really is love, then I would have to see this love in human flesh turning to victory the apparent defeat of all the martyrs. I would have to witness this love overcoming the meaningless death of countless sacrificial victims and conquering the tyranny of all our pain and grief. Before I could really believe that God is love, I would have to be able to stand by and watch this God suffer along with starving Ethiopians and Vietnamese boat people. Then, after every thing else, I would have to see Him rise above His own suffering.

Above all I knew that I would have to test the theory of divine love by examining the way that love worked itself out in my own life. I would have to experience love active in my own flesh and blood, conquering every hate and destroying every council of despair, for only then, without sentimentality or pretence, would I be able to join in the cry of the Sixties generation and once again shout their message from all the roof tops of the world:

"All you need is love."

BELIEVE IT OR NOT

"My Lord and My God!"

7

GOD IN THE FLESH

I never heard a French Republican cry out the name of "Napoleon Bonaparte" after striking his thumb with a hammer. Nor, in similar circumstances, do the English seem to be in the habit of calling upon "Winston Churchill". The Australians do not invoke the name of "Kylie Minogue" when roused to anger, and even the cult of Marilyn Monroe has never gone so far as to assume that her name has the power to curse as well as bless. Yet this is precisely what everyone seems to assume about Jesus, so that even the most militant non-believer shouts out his name when disaster strikes. What, I ask myself, is the power of Jesus' name that both Christian and non-Christian alike hold him in such awe and reverence?

Having asked myself for years why the name of Jesus still stands out above all other human names even in a non believing age like ours, I have finally been forced to conclude that the Christian answer, no matter how improbable it may seem, is the only one that makes any sense. For two thousand years Christians of every persuasion have been insisting that at a particular moment of history, in an outpost of the ancient Roman empire, there was a Jewish man who was also the Jewish God of sacrificial love. Out of envy he was killed by the local government authorities late on a Friday morning, but then overcame death by coming back to life the following Sunday. Christians further claim that He is still alive in a way so powerful that no one can remain indifferent to him forever. Either he really is the Jewish God of sacrificial love living in our human flesh or else he is the greatest fraud ever perpetrated on the human race.

When I first began to ask myself if Jesus was really God, I assumed that I would have to choose between him and some other human God such as Buddha or Mohammed. But then I discovered that throughout the entire course of human history Christians are the only people who have ever claimed that their founder was God Almighty. Though other peoples have treated certain powerful and influential human beings as if they were divine, this was only because they thought there was a spark of the divine in everyone anyway. And even at those moments in their history when the Romans treated Caesar as some kind of god, they never thought he was their creator and redeemer.

Platonists never fell down in adoration before Plato nor, until influenced by the Christian West, did Buddhists send out missionaries to tell others about a divine Buddha. Mohammedans never claim that Mohammed was Allah in the flesh, and even to hint at such a thing would be the height of blasphemy. Yet this is what Christians have always said about Jesus. If I want to find God in the flesh I do not have to choose between Jesus and some other claimant to the title. Jesus of Nazareth is the only human being anyone has ever claimed to be the one and the same God who made me and the whole universe. No other religion or philosophy has ever even conceived such a wild and preposterous idea.

I next discovered that this claim about Jesus was first made by the most unlikely people in the world ever to think that any human being could possibly be God. Unlike the pagans who imagined that their gods often walked about disguised as men and women, the Jews insisted that nothing on earth could ever represent God, whether disguised or not. Certainly no human being could ever be

God, and to suggest such a thing was even more repugnant to the Jews than it would be to a modern Moslem. Unlike their Roman conquerors who thought that the whole world was more or less divine, the Jews, as we have seen, were convinced that God was completely unworldly. If anyone went around acting as though he was God Almighty they would not have laughed him out of court as we might today. Instead they would have dragged him into court and condemned him to a traitor's death.

Jesus Himself was put to death precisely because he talked and acted as though he was God Almighty, and those who stayed with him to the very end, in spite of their Jewish background, were finally forced to believe that in some wonderful and mysterious way Jesus really was God in the flesh. He did those things only God could do, driving out evil spirits and forgiving sins, creating wine out of water, controlling thunder storms, and finally rising from the dead.

Unlike the neighbouring pagans who would have simply added Jesus to their list of gods and then carried on with life as though nothing had happened, the Jews had no idea what to make of him. "What manner of man is this", they asked, "that even the wind and the waves obey him?" And again, "We have never seen the likes of this before in all Israel, that the lame walk and the blind see."

The Jews were not gullible people. Unlike so many people today, and the pagans of an earlier age, they did not demand a miracle every time something went wrong in their lives. Nor did they expect divine thunderbolts to come suddenly crashing down upon the heads of their enemies, as much as they sometimes wished they might. You would never have caught the Jew with a rabbit's foot in his pocket or a horoscope on his bedside table, and even a king as powerful as King Saul was in serious trouble when he called up a witch from the dead in order to have his fortune told. The pagan saw himself caught up in the unpredictable events of an unscientific world, but, as we have seen, the Jew looked for order in the midst of the world's chaos and saw the presence of

God more in ordinary everyday events than in the miraculous and spectacular. The Jews were far from being superstitious.

Yet even though the Jews did not expect God to step into world affairs every time they turned around, they did expect Him to send someone who would deliver them from the oppression of the pagan Romans. He had, after all, once sent Moses to deliver them from Egyptian tyranny, and then established the nation as a powerful and independent kingdom in the days of David and Solomon. Now, precisely because God is consistent in what He does, it seemed to make more and more sense for Him to restore this Jewish kingdom to its former glory, so that by the time Jesus arrived on the scene the Jews were expecting a descendant of King David to save them from the Romans, just as Moses had once saved them from an earlier oppressor. What never crossed their minds was that this "Messiah", or "Christ" as he was known in the Greek language, would turn out to be God Himself come to earth to save them from the tyranny of their own selfishness.

On that famous Palm Sunday before the Jewish Passover feast when Jesus made his triumphal procession into the Jewish capital, the crowds really thought he might be the Messiah they were waiting for. He was, as the gospel accounts make clear, a direct descendant of King David and the "pretender" to the Jewish throne. If he had just given the signal the people could have risen up against the hated Romans, driven them out of Palestine and proclaimed Jesus, the son of David, as their rightful King. What no one expected or wanted was that instead he would rise up against the temple, their greatest national shrine, harangue its leaders as though he was God Almighty, and then return to the country to have a quiet dinner with some of his closest friends.

This whole story of Jesus' triumphal march into Jerusalem reads rather like one of the "Tales of the Unexpected". But this is typical of Jesus. He is always doing the unexpected and then treating it as perfectly normal. When he is only twelve years old he acts surprised that his parents did not know that he had to spend his time in the temple going about his Father's business. In Cana of Galilee he acts as though everyone at the wedding feast should have expected the water to have turned into wine, and he seems taken by surprise that people are so amazed at his healing miracles.

It soon becomes clear that Jesus wants everyone to expect him to do the unexpected, and that by taking people by surprise he forces them to ask what kind of person he really is. "Where does this man come from?", they ask. "Whose son is he?" "Is he just one of the village lads, the local carpenter's son, or does he come from God?" The Jewish leaders claim they know the answer. They insist that they know where Jesus comes from and who his father is, whereas no one will know where the real messiah comes from. But to this Jesus declares that they have no idea who his real Father is and that if they did they would believe in him.

Jesus keeps pressing the point; "Who do men say that I am?", and again, "What do you think of the Christ; whose son is he?" And just as "Tales of the Unexpected" gives us an unearthly feeling about what is going on, so the same thing begins to happen to Jesus' closest followers. They start looking for some kind of unearthly explanation for the surprising things he says and does. Then, at long last, Peter comes up with the answer Jesus wants: "You are the Christ," he says, "the son of the living God". Finally, almost at the end of the story, Thomas, the sceptic, falls down at the feet of the risen Jesus and exclaims, "My Lord and my God!"

It is almost impossible for us to imagine how difficult it was for these first followers to decide that Jesus actually was God and the embodiment of all that is real and true. Having been raised as orthodox Jews they knew that there could only be one God, and that if Jesus was God, he and the Father had to be one and the same God in much the same sort of way that my children and I belong to the same family. To be the son or the daughter of a Heidt is also to be a Heidt, everyone equally a Heidt, no one before or after another. This is how these first Christians gradually came to understand Jesus. He was "God from God, Light from Light, true God from true God". Though as a human being he was not as great as God the Father, as Son of God he was His Father's equal.

Because most of the Jews could not accept Jesus as their Lord and God, they ended up choosing the tyranny of Rome instead. When the moment of truth came, during Jesus' trial, they renounced their ancient inheritance and national independence, crying out in a single voice, "We have no king but Caesar". In a somewhat similar way I began to see that my own decision about Jesus would determine whether I would become a radical nonconformist able to stand up against the expectations and demands of modern society or continue to live under the tyranny of all the social attitudes with which I grew up. If Jesus really is God as well as a human being like myself, then I would have to do my best to see that all my attitudes and standards of behaviour came from him rather than from the world around me. I would be able to stand up against the world because I would have a place to stand that is not of this world. But if, on the other hand, I decide that he is simply a human being like myself and everyone else, then God has not come into my world and I can have no standards of behaviour apart from my own private prejudices and those of the society in which I live.

It was just as important for me to decide on the true identity of Jesus as it was for the ancient Jews. As the answer they gave affected all the rest of their history as a nation, so I knew that my answer would affect my whole outlook on life and everything I did from that moment on. If in Jesus God has become a human being like me, then not only will he give me a place to stand, but my own humanity will reflect something of what God is like, and the suffering of Jesus upon the cross, together with all the rest of the world's suffering, will reveal something of my own character as well as God's . Far from being just some ancient miscarriage of justice, the crucifixion becomes the sacrificial love of God worked out in human flesh. In the dark light of the cross my own life suddenly takes on a new significance and my suffering is radically transformed into a potential power for good.

I could see that if I accepted the crucified Jesus as God in the flesh my suffering would become worthwhile and my whole life infinitely valuable. But how could I possibly know for certain that He really is God? What evidence do I have? That there was once someone called Jesus who lived in a small country on the eastern shore of the Mediterranean some 2,000 years ago, now seems as certain as that Caesar lived in ancient Rome or Napoleon in Paris. Even though we cannot compare his writings with those of Caesar because he never wrote anything, nor venerate his tomb as we can venerate the tomb of Napoleon because he no longer has a tomb, we can, nevertheless, get a very clear impression of what he was like from the writings of his contemporaries. From them we learn that the wisdom of his teaching and his seemingly miraculous activities attracted a great following among the ordinary people until, whilst still in the prime of life, the Jewish leaders handed him over to the Roman authorities to be executed.

This much both Christian and non-Christian generally accept, and I think it would be extremely foolhardy not to do so. Yet this does not answer the question of who Jesus really is. Was he simply a great charismatic teacher or was he God Almighty? And what about the stories of his miraculous birth, his walking on water and his raising people from the dead? Above all, did he actually come back to life himself after his public execution, as most of his followers have always insisted? All these extraordinary claims are the things I found most difficult to accept, though from the beginning I had to admit that he must have acted in a very extraordinary manner to have been remembered at all. He certainly is not remembered as a great intellectual or military leader nor even as an outstanding philanthropist, and yet he left an impression on his contemporaries that has captured the human imagination ever since.

Most of us have neither the time nor the inclination to search out all the historical evidence we need to understand why Jesus made such an impression on the people of his day. We can however get some first hand evidence of what Jesus supposedly said and did simply by reading the early records about him in the books of the New Testament.

At first I was rather put off from reading these books because I assumed that they were far too complicated for me to understand and the language much too old fashioned to mean anything to me. Then I gradually came to realise that whatever trouble I may have had reading the bible came from my own pre-conceptions and complicated ways of thinking. The bible was not all that complicated, but I was. My reading was coloured by all sorts of mutually contradictory images of Jesus that I had picked up over the years from my parents and friends and Sunday School teachers. There was Jesus meek and mild, but also Jesus the rebel kicking the money changers out of the temple. And then there was Jesus the simple story teller, a sort of Hans Christian Anderson of his day, yet who for some quite unnecessary reason gets himself into trouble with the authorities and is executed for treason.

The image of Jesus that most dominated my mind was that of a religious teacher and miracle worker who spent all his time going about doing good for others and then being executed for it. He was the sort of person we could all admire and perhaps even try to copy at times, but hardly someone we would think of as a close friend or invite to one of our dinner parties. This was the trouble with my image of Jesus. Instead of being a real flesh and blood person like myself, He was only a vague ideal, and a religious ideal at that.

If I was ever going to find out what Jesus was really like, I began to realize that I would have to rid my mind of all these images and start afresh. I tried the experiment of picking up a single book of the bible as though I had never heard of it before and knew absolutely nothing of what it was all about. I pretended I had gone into my local library and discovered some strange and esoteric book called "Good News" by an unknown author simply going by the name of Mark. Curiosity getting the better of me, I checked out this new discovery, took it home and read it all in one sitting. When I did I found a very different kind of book from any I had ever read before. To my surprise there was no physical description of the book's hero nor any account of his family background. There was not even any reference to his childhood nor description of his special interests, skills or hobbies. How he made enough money to support himself and his followers is never revealed. Instead, what I found was a picture of someone bursting in upon the scene of ancient Israel, driving out demons, healing the sick, and embellishing this highly dramatic activity with stories about God's compassion for the poor and His stern judgements upon the contemporary leaders of the nation. Here I had come across not so much a detailed biography as an impressionistic portrait of someone whose personality had obviously had a very deep effect upon the author.

This at least is what I found in the first half of the book. But in the second half everything suddenly changed. Without explanation the author moved from a general impression of Jesus' activities to a detailed eye witness account of his last week on earth. Then in the last chapter there is a brief and somewhat incomplete account of how this man supposedly came back to life, almost as though the author assumed that the reader already knew that he was alive.

What struck me most about this book was its ring of authenticity. The portrait of the main character was painted in a disarmingly unselfconscious style, with no attempt to persuade nor any apparent concern for accurate detail. It was written with an irrepressible exuberance, almost as though the author himself was surprised by what he was saying. Later, when I read other New Testament writings about Jesus, I found this same exuberance. Similar events and sayings were used in different ways and presented in different contexts as though the authors had a treasury of common memories which they had to put to paper as quickly as possible without any structure or pre-conceived plan. Events and sayings were told with a kind of machine gun rapidity as little vignettes simply laid before the reader without explanation or embellishment.

Why, I began to wonder, should this remarkable variety of authors bother to make up such a story, especially when so much of it is so hard to accept? And, I asked myself, what about all those contemporaries of Jesus who would have known if the events described in these books had been made out of whole cloth? When there were so many people wanting to stamp out the early Christian Movement surely some of them would have pointed out that the whole story was a pack of lies. Yet nobody ever did. Apparently everyone knew better than that.

As incredible as much of the story seemed, I could not dismiss it from my mind. Even if some of the details might be the embellishments of enthusiastic imaginations, I was forced to ask what kind of a man could create such enthusiasm among so many people. What was it about Jesus that made his followers put into his mouth such phrases as "The Father and I are one", or "He who has seen me has seen the Father"?

One thing was certain. No one was ever going to put phrases like that into my mouth. Should I start talking that way, my closest friends would certainly do their best to keep it quiet, knowing that if word went round I might easily be locked up in a psychiatric ward as a menace to society and a danger to myself. Occasionally I have come across people who have acted as though they thought they were God Almighty, and I have even met someone who actually claimed that he really was God in the flesh. He was not alone in this of course. Ever since Adam and Eve chose to be imperfect gods rather than perfect human beings, we have all been trying to play God in one way or another. Yet we can never quite bring it off, and this lies at the heart of our human problem. Instead of turning into gods we become fools at best and tyrants at worst.

Or in the case of the man I met who really believed he was God in the flesh, far from having a great following of people trying to convert the world to his cause, he was isolated in a padded hospital cell reserved for the criminally insane.

With Jesus the situation was obviously very different. Everyone seems agreed that he was neither a fool nor a criminal, and should I think he was one or the other I would be passing a moral judgement on myself rather than on him, for I would be calling evil what everyone else calls good and insane what everyone else calls sane.

Almost without realising it, I had at this point moved away from the common idea that Jesus was simply a very good man or an extremely wise teacher, and had come to see that that was the very last thing he could possibly be. Anyone who goes about appearing to bring people's friends and children back to life and then telling them that they should listen to him as though he was God Almighty, can hardly be considered either wise or good. People who try that sort of thing are either very bad or completely mad, and those who try to encourage their cause ought to be exposed as dangerous frauds.

Throughout the last 2,000 years people have been trying to do just that. Powerful governments have attempted to wipe out everyone who has believed in Jesus, and in a quieter but more insidious way scholars have done their best to explain away all the stories about him. Yet they continue to be told and the followers of Jesus continue to grow. Whilst governments fall and scholars keep changing their minds, the beliefs of his followers stand more firmly than ever and the Christian movement continues to grow more rapidly now than ever before. At the end of the day I found that the only explanation that seemed to make any sense of all these undeniable facts was that the New Testament writings really are fundamentally accurate portrayals of Jesus as he really was.

Who then was he? According to the gospel portrait he was an ordinary man very much like myself but with extraordinary powers for doing good. He healed the sick and drove out demons, and he spoke with a wit and wisdom far surpassing the leading intellectuals of his day. Yet he also claimed to be the direct descendant of King David and the rightful heir to the Jewish throne, ushering in a new kingdom far surpassing anything ever seen in David's time or any time since. His was to be a kingdom of God's reign on earth, a kingdom which was to come in all its power and glory once all the peoples and nations of the earth believed in him instead of believing in their own ancient gods.

As well as claiming to be a new king of a new kingdom, Jesus also kept doing things the Jews of his day believed only God had a right to do. He healed people on the Sabbath Day and told them that their sins were forgiven. He walked on water and calmed storms on the Lake of Galilee just as though he was the same God of the storm who had once led His people through the waters into freedom from their Egyptian masters. It was even said that he had raised people from the dead. All this was too much for the Jewish authorities, and finally, for the sake of the nation, they condemned this man who acted as though he was God Almighty by crying out, "We have heard the blasphemy". Then, to make the nation safe once more, he was executed on a Roman cross as a traitor to their traditions.

Hardly anyone has ever doubted that Jesus died on the cross that dark Friday afternoon outside the capital city of Judaea. The Jewish authorities even had a guard placed at his tomb so that his followers would not steal his body away and claim that somehow or other he had been raised from the dead. Yet the body has never been found and no-one has ever venerated the tomb as his final resting place. Throughout the centuries people have tried to explain this away, and even now, almost twenty centuries later, someone has come up with the idea that instead of dying he actually fled to India where he lived to a ripe old age. But if you can believe something as unlikely as that, you might as well believe what the bible claims to have actually happened, that he died and was buried and rose again on the third day.

Here, it seems to me, are the actual facts in the case. If I accept them Jesus becomes the ultimate disclosure of who God really is and what He is like. He becomes the embodiment of all that is real and the key for finding some real meaning and significance in my life. I either believe that Jesus is God in the Flesh, or ignore him at my peril.

If I do not accept Jesus as my God, what other alternatives do I have? I am not likely to add my name to the dying breed of militant atheists, and I have no inclination to make up a new religion of my own. Instead I would have to join the ranks of all those secular pagans who subject themselves to the arbitrary whims of the gods of the modern world, be they wealth or prestige, power, security or sex. And then, when these gods betray me just as surely as they betrayed my pre-Christian ancestors, I would have to turn my back on them and probably join some sort of alternative life style community as a slightly old-fashioned hippie or modern revolutionary. In trying to find some kind of personal salvation, I might even dabble in the occult for awhile, or adopt the spiritual isolation of Eastern mysticism and the esoteric techniques of transcendental meditation. Then again I might simply experiment with alternative medicine or with the latest DIY fitness fad of the West. I have no idea which of these alternatives I might choose if I were not a Christian, but they seem to be about the only alternatives open to me, and I must confess that none of them has much appeal.

From the sheer force of the evidence I have decided instead to follow the way of Jesus rather than the way of secular society, and in doing so I have not simply exchanged a modern paganism overwhelmed by a richness of gods I can well do without for a Christianity bereft of all but a single god. Unlike the pagan trying to live out his life as best he can in a world of mysterious forces and warring gods beyond his comprehension or control, I have discovered in Jesus that behind and beyond the gods there is a divine personal community which is the unifying strength of all personal relationships. Jesus is the ultimate power of sacrificial love and the source of a peace which passes all earthly understanding.

By accepting Jesus I have learned that the godhead is not an army of divinities vying for power amongst themselves nor some isolated individual hoping that we will all share in His eternal loneliness. The God revealed in Jesus Christ is not simply a unit but a perfect unity of divine persons bonded together by sacrificial love. Not an integer but an integrated community in which there are no stresses, strains or tensions. Here I found a radical understanding of community life which the world had never known before. By immersing myself in a community of love I saw that my freedom would be enhanced and that by losing my life for the sake of others I would actually find it.

I learned this new understanding of community life from the cross, for there I saw the sacrificial love of God being worked out in the language of earthly flesh and human sin. In the cross I saw suffering and death sharing in the explosive energy of divine love. Then I knew why it had become for so many the symbol of life instead of a cruel instrument of execution, a decoration to be worn as a medallion round the neck and a sign of victory to be lifted high in the streets of our cities and over the altars of our churches. I saw that victory really can come out of suffering, and new life out of death.

Yet the cross by itself can give no assurance of love any more than death automatically leads to life. Other peoples have dreamt their dreams of life after death, and the world is strewn with the dead bodies of those who have given themselves to others out of loyalty and love. Yet only in Jesus do the dreams become real and the bodies return to life, for it was not the cross itself that brought new hope to the world but Jesus' victory over the cross.

To believe in the triumph of sacrificial love I knew that I would actually have to see new life coming out of death and new joy out of suffering. Otherwise the cross would be just another illustration of the sadistic nature of mankind and a road leading us into bondage to anyone who would take advantage of our devotion and play upon our loyalties. Only when the followers of Jesus saw that he was able to rise above death were they able to cry out with him, "Oh grave where is your victory? Oh death where is your sting?"

Believe It or Not

Transformation

8

Jesus' Uprising

When I was growing up the natural sciences fascinated me more than any of my other studies. I devoured every book I could find on geology, astronomy and basic physics, and I used to sit for hours imagining dinosaurs crashing through prehistoric forests whilst little horses, no bigger than my pet dog, played about my feet and giant dragon flies whirred above my head. In my mind's eye I could see that first stupendous moment when a solitary fish lugubriously crawled out of his watery environment to breathe air for the first time. Inwardly I honoured him for that daring act which eventually led to Michaelangelo and Einstein, space travel and, alas, the atomic bomb. Yet there was something I could never figure out about that gracious fish who took such a giant step on the evolutionary ladder of biological progress. Though I could appreciate his foolhardy audacity in climbing onto the beach in the first place, I could never figure out how he was able to survive once he got there. Wherever did he get the lungs that made it possible for him to breathe this new rarefied air?

In spite of all I have learned since about evolution, I still cannot figure it out. According to Darwin's original theory, animals and plants very slowly and almost imperceptibly developed new organs and other physical characteristics by adapting to their local environment. Dogs learned to bark to scare off enemies and fish developed fins in order to swim. But why, I wondered, should a fish develop lungs to breathe an atmosphere he had not yet encountered and adapt himself to an environment that had nothing to do with his own watery world? It seemed obvious to me that when that first fish moved out of the water to breathe the air of dry land, the earth was not witnessing another stage in a slow evolutionary development but a radical and revolutionary change in its entire way of life.

The theory that everything, including the human race, slowly evolved from simpler forms of life without any sort of dramatic or traumatic upheaval, was, as I now know, extremely reassuring to the people of Darwin's day. Following the upheavals of the French Revolution the notion of change or progress through slow gradual evolution involving almost imperceptible growth rather than through political revolution or biological upheaval appealed to people everywhere and especially to the English. What the Victorians ignored, however, and what biologists have since recognized, is that there are sudden major jumps forward in biological development which raise life to new and unexpected levels. Some creatures are suddenly able to do things never dreamt of before, though in hindsight we can see that the original creature had the potential for some such development. Fish, for example, had always been able to breathe, but suddenly one of them started to breathe in such a totally new and unexpected way that we now feel compelled to call it an amphibian instead of a fish. For some mysterious reason a wayward fish seems to have already adapted itself to a way of life he had never known and to an environment he had never experienced.

I cannot explain the mystery, for though species may develop by adapting to their present environment, this does not help me understand why a new kind of genus suddenly appears on the planet, nor by what means the first sea creature came to breathe air on dry land. All I know is that it could not just lay there on the beach waiting for its gills slowly but surely to turn into lungs, for, if it had, it would have been long dead before it ever took its first new breath. It had to have some kind of lungs before it needed them.

There are many sudden jumps like this in evolutionary progress which cannot be explained by gradual development, and among them is the unexpected appearance of men and women like ourselves. Though animals have always known all sorts of things, now all of a sudden one of them knows that he knows. He can put sentences together and make decisions for himself. Whereas before there was an animal living by instinct, now there is a person living by his understanding. Until that moment there may have been creatures very much like this first human being, but they were not the same. The first human being may likewise have been a very undeveloped human being but it was human nonetheless.

The first book of the bible is very clear about this, and I have always thought it made a great deal of sense. From purely scientific reasoning we cannot say, of course, that at a particular moment in the history of our planet Adam and Eve suddenly appeared as its first human beings. We may, if we wish, believe that two other people appeared instead whose names we do not know. Or perhaps several people suddenly appeared at the same moment in different parts of the world, though such an idea seems to stretch belief in coincidence almost to the breaking point. What we do know is that at a particular moment in time a new genus of animal, who for the first time could think reflectively and make free choices, suddenly appeared on the world scene where no such creature had been before. Call it mutation or divine creation or anything else, but the fact remains that human beings are qualitatively different from all that preceded them and so far are on the top rung of the evolutionary ladder.

Ever since I can remember, people have been trying to guess what the next step on this ladder of evolutionary progress is likely to be. The first theory I ever heard was that we would all eventually lose our little toes. Later, others who were perhaps a little more visionary suggested that our brains would get bigger and bigger so that we would be able to cope with all our new knowledge. Either theory may be true, I suppose, but I must admit that even though the outside toes on my own feet are not very large, I have no reason to believe that they are any smaller than those of my grandfather or even of my prehistoric ancestors, and as for our brains, I sometimes wonder if they might actually be getting smaller. We certainly seem rather short on Platos and Michaelangelos these days. The important question, however, is not how our race may gradually lose a few toes or grow bigger brains. What most of us want to know is what kind of superior creature, enjoying a completely new quality of life, may suddenly spring from our race just as we first sprang from the apes.

For the last 2,000 years Christians have been saying that this superior creature has already arrived on the scene. They claim that when Jesus crashed through the earthly limitations of human life by rising from the dead, a radical change in human development took place, so that even though there was an obvious continuity with the Jesus everyone had known before, a new man rose up out of the tomb capable of living a new form of life. In the uprising of Jesus a giant step in human development occurred which no-one had expected and which for most people still seems beyond belief.

People find it easy enough to believe that after a false trial based on trumped up charges Jesus was executed for treason by the Roman authorities for supposedly claiming that he, rather than Caesar, was the true king of the Jews. Most people however find it much more difficult to believe the further claim that early on the first day of the following week he was seen to be alive again.

I suppose our attitude towards the resurrected Jesus is not dissimilar to what most of those ancient fish still swimming about in the sea must have felt about the first amphibian. The vast majority probably saw this new land creature as nothing more than a fish out of water, and believed that those who followed him were mere misfits trying to live above their station. Undoubtedly many of them would have denied that land creatures even existed.

Yet on that day when the first fish breathed a radically new kind of air, I can imagine the stars singing out in wild anticipation and the entire universe trembling in awe at a new development which would some day give birth to creatures like you and me. Here was a fundamentally new creature, yet one which had developed from the old. Here was a creature which had begun its life as a fish and still retained characteristics of a fish, but which had been so transformed that it could rise above all the limitations of its original environment.

So it was with Jesus. He was always fully human, and when he rose from the grave he was as human as ever. But now he enjoyed a new form of life capable of living in an heavenly environment. Before he was crucified he had the natural capacity to live somewhat above his bodily and earthly limitations, but after the resurrection he was able to do so completely.

Contemporary witnesses insist that they did not just see a ghost that Sunday morning and the weeks following, but a living man who could eat and drink and still had the wounds of the crucifixion in his hands and feet. Yet he did not seem to be limited by his body, or by his physical environment, in any way. He would simply appear unexpectedly in the middle of a room, say or do something, and then just as unexpectedly disappear again.

One of the odd things about this "new man" was that his closest friends often failed to recognize him when he first appeared. In the garden where he had been buried Mary Magdalene thought that the person she was talking to on that first Easter morning was the gardener. She only realized that it was Jesus when he called her personally by name, as he had undoubtedly done many times in the past. Something similar happened later that same day when two of his followers were walking to the small town of Emmaus a few miles outside Jerusalem. They were joined by Jesus on the road but did not realize who it was until they arrived home together. There Jesus blessed and broke the bread at the beginning of their evening meal and in that breaking of bread they suddenly recognized him. They had been talking to Jesus all along and did not know it. Then once the truth dawned on them, he disappeared. The same thing happened a few days later when some of his former disciples went fishing. They looked up from their work to see a mysterious stranger sitting on the shore, but only after they went to the shore themselves and the stranger fed them some of his own fish, did they realize that here again was Jesus. It seemed you never knew if he might be present, and only when his apostles are all gathered together as in the upper room, is he recognized immediately.

It is as though his physical appearance signals his personal presence, but this presence can only be recognized by those who are clearly very close to him personally, or who share a common meal of fish or bread with him or are assembled together as his church. It was as though this new man could be with his followers in a variety of physical forms through which they could gradually come to see him as he really is. Not only a physical body but a common meal and the community of his faithful followers were all outward and visible signs of his inward and personal presence.

Jesus had prepared his immediate followers for something like this the night before he died. Blessing bread and wine at their last evening meal together, he told them that this was his body and his blood, and then added that in the future they should also bless bread and wine as he had done, to make him present with them again. "Do this", he said "for the re-calling of me." Here was a new way in which he would be physically with them until the end of time. But it was not the only way. After his resurrection he seemed to take the physical form of other human beings such as that of a gardener or of a stranger on the road to Emmaus and later his followers came to discover that he was personally present in each of them and that, to the extent that they were all filled with his Holy Spirit, they could recognize him in one another. Soon St Paul was talking about the church itself as Jesus' body, and Jesus himself is reported to have said that what they did to the least of his brothers they did to him.

What we seem to be witnessing here is a mutation in the evolution of life on earth by which the personal gains complete control over all its material environment including the biological components of its own body, so that Jesus' body now becomes a perfect expression of his own personality. This new "personalized body", or what the bible calls a "spiritual body", is a much more radical stage in the evolutionary process than either the former transformation of chemical elements into life or of fish into land animals, or even of mammals into reflective human beings. Yet no matter how radical it may be it is not inconsistent with what has gone before. From our perspective we may call it a move from the natural to the supernatural or from the personal to the super personal, but seen from the perspective of the final goal of the whole evolutionary process this further development in human life is the most natural of all, for it is the final fulfilment of all that life was capable of becoming in the first place.

The transformation of Jesus' earthly body into his resurrected body is not inconsistent with the kind of change that took place in those first fish who rose from the sea to the land and later from land into the air. Just as there was something about some of the sea creatures which made it possible for them to develop lungs which could breathe the air of dry land, so there must be something about us which makes it possible for us to live a resurrected life. We only discovered that we could live this kind of life however, when Jesus actually rose from the dead, just as it was only after one of the sea creatures actually found itself on dry land and started to breathe air for the first time that land animals were able to cover the earth. The new resurrected Jesus shows us that our dreams of glory can come true, and that there is something about us that makes it possible to live a greater life than we would ever have thought possible.

Yet we cannot do this by our own efforts nor live this kind of life by our own power. Someone other than ourselves must raise us up to inaccessible heights, just as Jesus, though he had the inherent capacity to rise from the dead, could only do so through the creative power of God. We can live a new kind of life, but we can no more create that new life for ourselves than bricks and mortar can turn themselves into a new house.

When I was still in the early stages of my Christian pilgrimage I could fairly easily believe that Jesus had become some new kind of human being after his resurrection, but I failed to see how that could possibly make any difference to my own life. There is after all a world of difference between believing that a long time ago one particular man happened to come back to life after he died, and discovering that my own dearest friend who recently died of cancer has come back to life. If I found my friends regularly rising from the dead the creative energy of God's sacrificial love would be fairly evident, but the claim that once upon a time a single person rose from the dead is no evidence at all. Even if Jesus really did rise from the dead the fact seems so out of keeping with all the rest of our experience as to be quite irrelevant.

Then I came to realize that the resurrection of Jesus initiated a change in the whole ecological balance of creation which deeply affected not only my own life and the society in which I live but the entire material world as well. It was a radical new step in a revolutionary process of transformation which had begun well before the birth of Jesus. When we ourselves first evolved from lower forms of animal life and then domesticated some of the very animals from which we evolved, we turned life on our planet upside down and perhaps changed the future development of the entire universe. Now Jesus completes this transformation. "Behold", he says, "I make all things new". His resurrection ushers in a new era of earthly life in which not only his fellow human beings, but all created things have the possibility of living a new kind of life in a new environment. For the first time everything is free to be completely true to itself, stripped of all those limitations hindering its full development. Here is nothing short of a new creation or re-creation which Jesus inaugurates by his own resurrection. From then on a "new heaven and a new earth" is in the making, and Jesus becomes "the first fruits of them that sleep."

This transformation operates through the power of the Holy Spirit sent into his church by Jesus after the resurrection. For some time after that first Easter morning his followers never knew when Jesus might suddenly appear, but once they became used to the idea, he said he was leaving their sight for good. Yet, through his Holy Spirit he would be with them until the end of time and would make it possible for them to continue his work on earth, even going so far as to say that they would do greater works than he had done.

It is through this same Holy Spirit that we continue to take part in the new resurrected life of Jesus and become his new earthly body. All of us are born with dreams of future glory we never achieve, and a craving for an eternal life we know will be destroyed by death. But our bodies simply cannot support our wildest dreams. Instead they gradually drag us down to the grave and kill all hope of immortality. After Jesus rose from the dead however, death itself was transformed into the gate of life. In our deaths we now share in his death, and through his crucifixion rise with him in glory. By his resurrection our deaths become the means of our perfection and fulfilment, our dreams of glory mere intimations of our own future resurrection. Death is revealed as the final step in our pilgrimage from earthbound limitations to a glorified freedom.

Death completes a process of transformation which begins with the death of self-will and self-centredness. As we die to ourselves we are filled with the supernatural energy of sacrificial love, and a life of limitless power begins to work in us, gradually helping us realize that we are made for better things than a life limited by the confines of mere earthly power. We are able to develop new lungs for breathing a new kind of air, spiritual lungs which are able to breathe in that Holy Spirit Jesus promised to give his followers.

God initiates people into a new human environment where their ability to breathe in the Holy Spirit gradually develops to the point where they are able to live the resurrected life of Jesus himself. The outward sign of this initiation is baptism, and in the breaking of bread, or Holy Communion, we actually take part in the resurrection of Jesus. We eat and drink his resurrected body and blood, so that they may infuse our own natural body and blood with the power of his resurrection. We gradually grow out of our earthly limitations through a process known technically as sanctification which, as I found out to my surprise, simply means being true to one's self. By growing in sanctity or holiness we develop the spiritual organisms for living in the new supernatural environment for which we were originally made.

Growth in sanctity however, can be a very frightening experience, as I soon found out. Like those original fish who found themselves on dry land we are not sure we can survive in the rarefied air of this new environment. Almost from habit we keep trying to breathe in the Holy Spirit with our own natural hearts and minds which have been designed only for earthly everyday life. Then, when we discover this does not work, we become frightened or discouraged and, as so many of those earlier creatures must have done, we scuttle back to our old familiar environment where we feel safe and secure. Like the ancient Jews led out of the confines of Egypt by Moses, we cry out, "Why have you led us into this wilderness to die?".

Some people do learn to breathe this new air quite freely and easily, and many of us have had the experience of doing so even if only for very short periods of time. We have had a foretaste of a life of personal freedom and of a power and energy beyond the possibilities of our own natural resources. We discover that we know more than we had ever been taught, that we can endure the unendurable and achieve the impossible. When we give up all our attempts to save ourselves and simply let the new life which comes from prayer and sacraments permeate our entire personality, we discover that far from dying we start to live a kind of life we could never have imagined before.

Our only immediate evidence for the resurrection is the community of the faithful where people continually scuttle back and forth between the new creation and the old. The practising Christian is both Superman and Clark Kent. The latter we can easily understand for he is of the natural order of things, another ordinary human being like ourselves with all our weaknesses and failings. Superman on the other hand is a mythical figure representing our dreams of glory, a sign of our belief that somehow or other we were made for greater things than our ordinary natural powers make possible. In himself he is but a creature of our own imagination, but if from time to time we actually see Clark Kent turning into Superman, no matter how infrequently, then we know that a supernatural resurrection really must have happened and that we too are capable of living a life greater than our natural powers will allow.

Among the followers of Jesus we discover people already living this new kind of supernatural life. Not only are there people like Mother Theresa who have a power for good beyond any natural explanation, but all those thousands living in our own villages and towns whose sufferings make their simplest actions super-heroic acts of virtue. Then there are those many people who whilst still on earth have displayed various characteristics of Christ's resurrected body, such as Blessed Martin of Porres who loved the sick and dying so much that he was seen looking after them all over the world, even though it is well attested that he never left his monastery in Peru. Others like St Francis of Assisi, or Padre Pio in this century, have had such great love for Jesus that they have actually carried in their own bodies the wounds of his crucifixion, and still others have had remarkable healing powers or have become so united to the resurrected Christ in prayer that their bodies have defied the normal laws of gravity.

When Jesus rose from the dead the mythical hope of all mankind became historic fact for the first time, and down the ages this same fact has continued to be multiplied in the resurrected lives of his followers. In rising from the grave Jesus inaugurated a general uprising of all mankind and set in motion a new revolutionary movement of the human spirit that is gradually transforming not only mankind but the entire universe into the resurrected body and blood of our God. Here is a revolution in human history far greater than any revolution ever conceived by the most radical politician or social reformer, a revolution which no tyranny can suppress for long, a perpetual revolution which shall only be completed when this era of earth's history comes to an end and there is a new heaven and a new earth, which shall themselves be the perfected body and blood of Christ risen from the shackles of our present death ridden lives.

BELIEVE IT OR NOT

Seeking the Invisible Man

9

The Invisible Man

Those who already accept Christianity anyway, may well believe that some kind of revolution of the human spirit is taking place in their lives. Are there enough signs however, of such a revolution in the lives of ordinary Christians to convince anyone else that the power of Jesus risen from the dead really is at work in the world? If not in his followers, where else can we possibly find this power?

Most of the Christians I have met do not really seem to expect me to find the living Jesus in them anyway, and rarely, if ever, talk about Jesus in a personal way, only referring to him occasionally as "The Lord" in the most non-committal manner imaginable. In my search for the living God it is probably quite safe for me to ignore them all together as they are not likely to convince me about Jesus or anything else for that matter. There are some Christians though, especially those of the more evangelical type, who go around talking about Jesus as though he was one of their most intimate friends and suggest that at any moment he might become my intimate friend as well. I find that Christians who talk like this seem to be totally unaware of the real problem they pose for me, for they do not seem to realize that claiming to have some special personal relationship with a man who died two thousand years ago cannot possibly help me get on intimate terms with him today. Though I can sympathize with anyone who feels close to the dead, it does not make me close to them as well, and it is no good pointing out that one particular man rose from the dead and is alive and well today. That may be fine for those who believe in him anyway, but if I cannot see him he might just as well be dead. There is no way I can get to know Jesus if I cannot meet him, and so far he has not walked up and introduced himself to me as my personal friend and saviour. Nor, in spite of what others have told me to expect, does he seem likely to do so.

It is all very well for Jesus to have told doubting Thomas, "Happy is the man who has not seen me and yet believes", but if this is what my happiness depends upon I may just have to resign myself to being miserable. I cannot see myself getting nearer to placing my faith in an invisible God by first being asked to believe in an Invisible Man. Christian enthusiasts seem to be asking the impossible when they tell me to believe in someone I have no hope of ever meeting face to face. As Jesus himself said, "How can you love God whom you have not seen if you do not love your brother whom you have seen?"

I realize, of course, that there are all sorts of things we believe in that we will never be able to see. I have never actually seen my wife's honesty, but I believe in it because I have seen countless signs that she is honest. Though I have never actually seen the wind, I would be a fool to disbelieve in hurricanes when I see all the damage they cause. In the same sort of way I suppose I could believe that an Invisible Man is walking beside me, but only if some unseen force knocks my hat off or taps me on the shoulder. Just as a blind man is likely to become aware of my presence only after I touch him or speak to him, so I can appreciate that all of us are blind when it comes to Jesus. All this means however, is that I will only be able to believe in him if things happen to me which cannot be explained in any other way.

There is, of course, another reason for believing in all sorts of things we never actually see. I believe that there really is a place called China, even though I do not have any hope of ever going there myself, because I trust those who claim to have been there. For a similar reason I also believe there was once someone called Napoleon. Historians who have read Napoleon's letters and studied the writings of those living at the time have told me about him, and I think I would be extremely foolish to doubt what they say. I admit then, that when I am looking for visible signs of an Invisible Man, I will have to take into account the evidence of those who claim they have been touched by him, and the testimony of writers who insist they saw him in the flesh.

But what visible signs and personal testimony are there that Jesus, the Invisible Man, is at work in the world today? I find very few. There is first of all the bible which claims to report the sayings and actions of Jesus whilst he was visibly present on earth. Then there is the church which maintains by its teachings and rituals that Jesus is still among those believers who gather together in his name. Finally there is the witness and lifestyle of those who claim that Jesus has actually come into their lives. That seems to be about it. If I examine the bible, the church and the lives of ordinary Christians, yet cannot find good enough reasons in any of these to convince me that there really is an Invisible Man called Jesus who is alive and active on earth today, then I might as well abandon my quest for the supreme invisible God and make do as best I can with everyday life as I find it. I will have to learn to be satisfied with the gods of power, ambition and material pleasure which I can see, rather than waste my time pursuing the will-o'-the-wisp search for a God I cannot see.

As for the bible, few people today have any first hand knowledge of what it says, although most everyone seems to have heard just enough about the findings of biblical critics to think that it is quite unreliable for proving anything. Even less people have any idea of what the church actually teaches, and from newspapers and television programmes they have the impression that the church is not quite sure it has anything to teach at all. About the only contact most people have these days with the church's rituals are an occasional attendance at baptisms, weddings or funerals, which they are not likely to associate with the active presence of a living God. It would seem, therefore, that we cannot expect much either from the bible or from the church in our search for the Invisible Christ. We will have to rely almost entirely upon our personal contact with people who go to church and consider themselves Christians. So let us begin with them to see if their lives give us any reason for believing that Jesus is actually at work in the world today.

When I look at most Christians the first thing I notice is that their Christian belief seems to have made almost no difference whatsoever to their personality or lifestyle. Apart from talking about religion or the church they appear to be just like everyone else. The only difference that I can see between these self-confessed Christians and other people is their claim to be Christian. Take that away and nothing changes. They may be pleasant or irritating, left or right wing in their politics, careless in their personal habits or over fastidious, but whatever style of life they lead or general convictions they hold the Christian Faith seems to have had little to do with it. In all fairness most of these committed Christians do seem to be rather good people, especially if judged by middle class standards, but then so are a great many others who have no Christian belief at all. In spite of their middle class standards, I fail to find any significant evidence that Jesus has transformed their lives in any way.

There are exceptions, of course. The beliefs of some Christians appears to have affected just about everything they do, to the extent that the only thing they seem able to talk about is Jesus Christ and what he has done for them. But my trouble with these people is that, on the whole, I do not like what Jesus appears to have done. They all seem so earnest, always going about trying to do their best to help everyone, and giving the impression that the less enjoyment they get out of it the better it is. They are good people, but appear to spend most of their time and energy attempting to make everyone else as good as they are, and criticising all those who do not come up to their own standards.

This is not the picture of Jesus that I get from reading the bible. I cannot imagine these modern Christians hanging about, as Jesus did, with thieves and prostitutes and all kinds of disreputable people. They seem much too concerned about getting people to give up things like smoking to think about that sort, and though I do not think smoking is a very good thing, I am not going to bother placing my faith in someone who supposedly died and rose again simply to help us break the habit. Nor am I going to be interested in such a person if the chief purpose of his work was to bolster up current middle class values. In England we have recently had a prime minister quite capable of doing that herself, and we have hardly needed a resurrected Christ to help her along. It is true of course that if we can convince enough people that Jesus is Lord and that, more than anything else, he wants people to be nice to one another it will considerably reduce the work of the police. But the last thing I personally want is to be associated with a group of people who think of themselves as some kind of celestial police force.

If, then, I look at the lives of the Christians I actually know for any real evidence of the transforming power of Jesus' resurrection, I find myself in an embarrassing situation. The Christians I like are those whose beliefs do not seem to make very much difference in their everyday lives, and the ones who claim that their lives are based entirely on their beliefs tend to be people I do not really care for very much and certainly would not want to be like.

Is there any hope then of finding the transforming power of Christ working within my friends and acquaintances? In spite of all the superficial appearances to the contrary, on reflection I have to admit that perhaps there is. I may have been a little too hard on these Christian friends and acquaintances who after all are weak, frightened, and insecure human beings just like myself. People do not suddenly cease to be human just because they become Christians. If they did there would be nothing about them which needed transformation. Most Christians, I find, do not claim that they have been changed overnight, but only that they have been given a new hope and a new strength in spite of their weakness and fears. They have a new life but the same old character as before, and like the first amphibians they continually scuttle back and forth between the two.

Perhaps the Christians I like the most are those I only see when they have scuttled back into the habits of their old untransformed character, whereas the ones I do not like may simply be living in a world I have not yet learned to appreciate. But in either type I have no idea what kind of change may have taken place over the months and years except for those few I have known well for a very long time. Unless I know what someone was once like I cannot imagine what kind of transformation may have taken place in his or her life, any more than I can recognize an acorn by looking at an oak tree. All I can do is compare the oak tree with greater and older oak trees nearby, and observe the damaged and broken branches that each tree has suffered as part of its continuous growth. So it is with my Christian friends. Whilst seeing how much they still need to grow, I also observe the scars and bruises they have already received as part of that growth so far. There may still be many things about them that I do not like, but I have no idea what they may have been like before, or for that matter what they may be like in the years to come.

Whether we are able to recognize the transforming power of Christ in people's lives depends, of course, upon what kind of transformation we are looking for. A young "punk rocker" in my parish who had recently been converted through an experience of Christ's transforming power was asked how he had changed since becoming a Christian. At first he replied that he didn't think he had changed at all, but then, on reflection, he added, "Yes I have. I am happier now." This is the promise Jesus held out for all of us. He died and rose again to make us happier, or more "blessed" as the older translations of scripture used to call it. Our "punk rocker" was happier because he now had a future. He had hope, and this hope gave him new energy and a new confidence. He still had the same basic character as before with his own particular personality. That had not changed. But he now had a new purpose in life and was gradually discovering a new power within himself that could overcome anything others might do to him. He no longer needed to defend himself from other people because he was no longer afraid of being humiliated or destroyed by them. Instead of fighting he could begin to love other people sacrificially without counting the cost. Those who now meet him for the first time find him a pleasant young man with a lot of personality and charm who is beginning to "grow up". Yet others who have known him well for a long period of time realise that a change has taken place which cannot be explained away by his background, environment or natural temperament. He has a faith anchored in a new hope which more and more expresses itself in sacrificial love.

I must confess that in a great many Christians I find a unique combination of faith, hope and love which I cannot explain by purely natural causes. When there is no clear evidence for faith, no basis for hope in a world like ours, and no grounds for believing that love will lead to anything but frustration and betrayal, I ask myself what justification there can possibly be for any of these attitudes. I certainly cannot write them off as so much sentimental nonsense, if for no other reason than that the people who are motivated by them tend to be no-nonsense sorts of people. Far from living in some make believe world of romantic fantasy, they are, as a whole, very practical down to earth people; just as much aware of the facts of life as I am, if not more so. With all their ideals and enthusiasms they may at times seem to have their heads in the clouds, but they also most certainly have their feet solidly on the ground. Their happiness is not due to some sort of whistling in the dark but to a power and energy far different from what one would expect in the kind of world we live in.

Just as the ancient Jews maintained that everything they knew about God came from God Himself, so these people insist that their happiness comes from the resurrected Jesus actually living within them. And, as with the Jews, I have come to find it extremely difficult if not impossible to find any other explanation. In spite of all their weaknesses and failings I have had to admit that in many ways the lives of my Christian friends really are outward and visible signs of the presence of the resurrected Christ and that Jesus the Invisible Man is actually visible in their faith, hope and love.

Even though this may be true of certain individuals, I have had to ask myself if it can also be true of the church as a whole. On the surface it would hardly seem so. Far from helping people believe in the powerful presence of Jesus, all too often it is the church which puts people off any kind of belief at all. If I look to the church for faith, I only find squabbles about doctrine and church leaders who seem to delight in publicising their doubts about everything. If I look for signs of hope I find a general retrenchment instead, combined with a general feeling of discouragement and discontent. If I look for love I find a closed and somewhat secret society in which people cling to one another and ignore everyone else - unless, of course, they can re-make everyone else into spiritual clones of themselves. Rather than a sign of the living Christ the church has all the appearance of a dying club existing though the sheer weight of its own inertia.

Where in the church can we possibly find the power of Jesus' resurrection or the happiness that is supposed to come from possessing it? Instead of power I see weakness, ineffectiveness, and despair, and when I look for happiness I find tense and earnest people eager to judge and criticise everyone different from themselves. The church is supposed to be Christ visible among us, the very body of Christ, according to St Paul. What kind of Christ do I see then, in a church where the signs of faith, hope and love seem so hard to find? Rather than a society of people animated by the Holy Spirit I find a rag-bag of weak, selfish and desperate people animated by the spirit of aggressive self-centredness pretending they have something special which no-one else really wants. I can, of course, appreciate the idea that people who accept Jesus Christ as the living God ought to belong to the church he started and get together on a regular basis with their fellow believers, but I find it very difficult to believe that this same church can give me any evidence that Jesus really is the living God.

The non-believer finds it extremely hard to understand how Jesus can be recognized in an institution dominated by people who do not seem to have ever been touched by him. So far I have only found one answer to this dilemma that has ever made any real sense to me. The story is told of a devout Christian in the late middle ages who, after trying to convert a wealthy Jewish friend for many years, had met with no success whatsoever. Then one day he learned to his dismay that this friend of his was taking a lengthy business trip to Rome. Surely, he thought, the corruption of the church in Rome would put him off Christianity forever. How great then was his amazement when this Jewish friend returned some months later a committed baptised Christian. Asked if he had seen all the corruption in the church, the Jew explained that that is precisely what had converted him. It seemed to him, and I must say that it seems to me as well, that any church which could survive that amount of corruption for 1600 years must be divine. That this same church today is not only still around 2,000 years after the crucifixion but actually thriving throughout the world in spite of continuous corruption from within and attack from without, must surely be one of the greatest signs of the living presence of the resurrected Christ there can possibly be. It seems obvious that without the risen power of Jesus the church would have been dead and buried long ago.

Yet, as much as the continuing existence of the church may demonstrate the reality and power of Jesus' resurrection, even more convincing to me is the fact that all the criticism we level against the church comes from the teaching of the church itself. Church people may not live up to Christian standards, but it is only because of the continuous witness of the church that we have these standards to live up to. Though the church's lack of faith, hope and love may keep us from believing in the resurrected Christ, it is only the church's teaching that ever made us realise the importance of these virtues in the first place. In a similar vein I may criticize the church for not being a very forgiving community but at least it teaches the importance of forgiveness, whereas a non-Christian culture like Japan does not even have any word for forgiveness.

I began to see why my Christian friends are able to be so completely loyal to the church on the one hand, whilst constantly criticizing it on the other. They realize that the church is a self-correcting community, continuously being reformed and renewed by its own faith in spite of the sins of all its members, and their very loyalty to this community drives them to take part in its self-correction. Far from depressing them as it might depress the outsider, the weakness and immorality of the church's members gives them some of their surest evidence for faith, for from these they know that the continuous spiritual power of the church and the high standards of its teaching could not possibly have come from itself and must therefore have come from the living God.

Yet the church is not our only evidence for faith. Reading the bible is also supposed to convince us of the presence of the risen Christ. Surely however this must depend upon who reads it. Highly educated people have just as frequently used the bible to disprove the resurrection as to prove it, and it is sometimes said that even the devil can quote scripture. I find that most people seem to use the bible as a collection of sayings they can haul out at any time to prove most anything they happen to like, whether it be genuine faith in God or their own private moral prejudices. Yet I feel sure that the bible was never meant to be a collection of proof texts handed down by God to be used as sledge hammers of debate for knocking down our opponents. From a cursory reading it soon seemed obvious to me that most of the passages in the bible could not be used to prove anything, and it was not long before I learned that far from being a collection of proof texts, the bible was a library of books chosen by the church to provide us with a record of one particular people's cultural history. The Jewish and Christian community compiled the bible by selecting a variety of writings from its most representative authors, and these were then said to be inspired by God precisely because the culture they represented was itself inspired.

In the bible I read about the same weaknesses and sinfulness I found in the church, and like the church in every age, I also found the action of God overriding this sinfulness and the power of God overcoming its weakness. In the bible I did not read the story of good people made better by their own inherent strengths, but of bad people being made good by God. By reading the bible to discern the action of God within the life of His chosen people, I also came to discover all that God has done for us. I came to realize that the common life presented in the bible is very much the same kind of life we find in the church today. Each presents us with the same evidence for the continuous action of the living God, and we cannot separate one from the other.

Some years ago the University of Chicago published a collection of books called *Great Books of the Western World*, containing the representative writings of Western civilization in the fields of poetry and fiction, physics and philosophy, history and art and just about everything else. Simply by reading these books someone from another culture could enter into the Western mind and learn what it is really like, and by absorbing the mentality of their authors could eventually become a Westerner. So it is with the bible. By reading the various books within it you and I can enter into the mind of the Jewish-Christian culture. We can become spiritual Jews, and, according to Christian belief, in doing so we will also enter into the mind of God.

This can only happen however if we read each book in the spirit in which it was written. We do not read a mystery book as though it were a law book, nor should we read a Jewish myth as though it were history nor an eye witness account of the crucifixion as though it were myth. As with any other book we might read, we need to ask what the author wanted to say when he wrote the way he did, and only then can we ask if what he wanted to say is true. In a mystery story where the suspect's alibi depends upon him being in another town on Friday the 13th of June 1983, it makes no difference to the point of the story whether there ever was such a day in that particular year or not. If, however, the story is really the account of an actual trial and it turns out that there was no Friday the 13th in June 1983, I should insist upon a re-trial. In the same sort of way the question we must ask of scripture is not whether it contains any errors, but whether or not the errors it contains are presented as though they were factually true.

If we find that no matter what errors there may be, the books of the bible present a continuous record of a people chosen by God for the salvation of the human race, and that one member of this people, Jesus of Nazareth, fulfils all their hopes and desires and continues to do so for people today, then we have the clearest evidence that God himself was behind the writings of these books.

In Christ's body, the church, no matter how corrupt it may be; in the lives of Christ's faithful people, in spite of all their sinfulness; and in the bible, whatever errors it may contain, I believe I have seen enough of the Invisible Man, Jesus Christ, to embark upon the journey of faith, and walk where millions have walked before.

BELIEVE IT OR NOT

The Faith that Begins in Dreams and Ends in Eternity

10

BEYOND BELIEF

The lives of individual Christians, the survival of the church, and the witness of scripture compelled me to take the first steps along the road of Christian faith in order to test the Christian claims by my own experience rather than dismiss them out of hand. Though all my questions are not yet answered, now that I have travelled that road for several years I am more convinced than ever that among all our contemporary ideas, philosophies and religious beliefs, Christianity makes the most sense of my own life and of the world in which I live.

By persevering in my quest for faith I believe that I have actually tasted and seen that the Lord is good. From time to time I have even experienced something of the power of the Holy Spirit working in my life. In all honesty I think I can now call myself a believing Christian, even though I may not be a very good one.

Nevertheless, I still have all sorts of prejudices which seem quite inconsistent with my Christian beliefs, to say nothing of the prejudices of all the people who continue to influence me. According to Christianity I am to do good to all men, but others tell me that God helps those who help themselves. Christian teaching urges me to adopt a spirit of poverty and humility whereas everyone else says that I should take more pride in myself and learn to stand on my own two feet. Most serious of all, even though traditional Christianity claims to be the full revelation of God, everywhere I go I am expected to assume that it is no better than any other religion.

These attitudes are all part of the collective insight of the culture in which I was raised, and their influence has been an essential ingredient in my own personal development. How, then, can I condemn them out of hand just because many of them do not happen to fit in with traditional Christian values and beliefs?

Why, after all, should these traditional beliefs necessarily be better than the common assumptions of my own culture or, for that matter, superior to the beliefs of other religions? I happen to be a Christian, but given the society in which I grew up there was little else I was likely to become if I was to become anything at all. Where I grew up Christianity, religion and goodness all meant practically the same thing. I still remember being amazed to learn as a young child that my Jewish friends, who seemed just as good as everyone else and were perhaps more devout than my own family, were not really Christians. Nevertheless everyone I knew, except for Jews, Communists and Atheists, tended to think of themselves as some kind of Christian even if they did not do much about it.

Just because Americans thought they were Christians however, did not necessarily make it right to be a Christian. Americans were definitely wrong about a lot of other things such as violence and Vietnam, and in spite of claiming to be a Christian country America certainly seemed to have more than its fair share of wickedness and greed. If, with all its non-Christian attitudes America was still Christian, it did not say very much about the superiority of Christianity over other cultural attitudes.

At the same time that I was questioning the Christian foundation of my own culture and its influence on my life, I began to discover all sorts of other cultures and beliefs which in many ways seemed just as attractive as Christianity, if not more so. I admired the American Indian's reverence for nature and even learned to respect the Hindu's sacred cows. I envied the family life of my Jewish friends and found greater peace in Hari Krishna than in the Christian Church and more zeal by far in Islam than in Christendom. Though I happened to be born into a culture where Christianity was the only obvious religious option, I was not so naive as to think that my own cultural background was necessarily better than that of the Jew or even the Buddhist.

How could I possibly believe that by some providential accident of birth I happened upon the one true faith, whilst everyone else had it wrong? And how, I began to wonder, should it be that my local parish church with its painfully boring services provided a more certain road to salvation than a Buddhist temple. Why should the Christian claim to a unique revelation make Christianity any better than those religions which only lay claim to a profound spiritual insight? I appreciated the fact that Christians alone believed that their founder was God incarnate, but I could not understand why belief in this incarnated God was necessarily any better than other people's belief in re-incarnated men and women.

Nor was it just this great variety of religious beliefs that made me wonder whether Christians could honestly lay claim to a special revelation from God. Within Christianity itself people believed so many different things that I did not see how I could possibly decide which beliefs had been revealed by God, and which had merely been made up during the last two thousand years. How was I to choose between Catholic and Protestant, Modernist and Fundamentalist, Traditionalist and Liberal? Should I eventually make a choice, how would I know that my choice was right or that my final belief alone was true? Perhaps the best I could do was to believe whatever I happened to like, and then own up to the fact that my beliefs were no better nor worse than those of anyone else.

In a world where television brings Buddhist temples and primitive religious rites directly into our sitting rooms when we least expect them, and where Irish Catholics and Protestants can kill each other before our very eyes, it would seem that the best thing we can do is learn how to live and let live and agree to disagree, accepting the rather illogical theory that what may be true for me is not necessarily true for anyone else.

At first I thought there was something quite wonderful about this new development in human consciousness. If, after all these centuries, we could at last give up insisting that we alone are right and that everyone else is wrong, bigotry might finally come to an end, and we all might learn to live together in peace and harmony for the first time. By some strange irony of history it began to look as though the peace we have all been looking for may not come from right belief but from agreeing that no-one's beliefs are necessarily right.

The only trouble with this simple solution to our religious differences, so far as I could see, was that I could not fit them in with my new found Christian faith, for though it allowed me to believe in Jesus Christ it did not allow me to believe in Him all that much. I could call him Lord and God all I wanted, but only in the same sort of way I could say that my wife was "simply divine". Yet I had come to realize by now that the whole point of believing that Jesus alone is God is that it had made it possible for me to put my entire faith in Him and in no-one else. I could no more call Him Lord and then treat him as just one of the pagan gods or Jewish prophets than I could believe in my wife's honesty and yet accept my friend's claim that she is a thief and a liar.

Having finally come to believe in the Christian Faith it began to look as though I was now being asked not to believe very much in anything at all, searching after the truth without ever hoping to find it. Accepting what everyone else believed - except the belief that their beliefs might actually be true. If all truth is relative and beliefs are formed more by cultural conditioning than by divine revelation, then the wisest course of action is to get on with life as best we may, and set aside the desire to be right as the relic of a more primitive and superstitious age.

At this stage in my pilgrimage of faith I suddenly woke up with a start to realize that far from abandoning the convictions of a more primitive and superstitious age, I had ended up right back in that primitive mentality from which I had tried to escape. Having travelled the long and difficult road towards Christian belief, I suddenly found myself once more in the quicksands of a dogmatic scepticism where nothing is right or wrong but only thinking makes it so. I found myself once again thrown into that battle of the gods where the honest convictions of others and the pressures of everyday life threatened to tear me apart. Yet it was precisely to escape this unending conflict and morass of uncertainty that I had originally come to place my faith in a God who had revealed Himself to His chosen people.

It now seemed as though my quest for faith had been wasted and my desire for truth misguided. Apparently, if I was to live in peace with my fellow human beings, I did not dare believe that a divine revelation had really been revealed nor that my membership in the Christian Church should be taken all that seriously. In the name of some new kind of Christian charity which I could not easily understand, I was expected to defend the beliefs of those who denied my own and embrace the enemies of Christ as long lost friends in the faith.

I was being asked to join the modern sceptic who, like the ancient pagan, rarely if ever asks if his religious beliefs are actually true and as a whole thinks that such questions are rather pointless. For him religious truth is something discovered or even invented rather than revealed. He embraces a practical wisdom developed over the centuries to help him deal with everyday life as best he can, whereas I had come to accept that there really has been a divine revelation and that I belonged to a people who had an understanding of reality and human life which could only have come from God Himself. How then was I to put my faith in this revelation and, at the same time, not only live in peace with those whose beliefs were radically different from my own but actually respect and appreciate their beliefs? How, in other words, could I believe that I was right without thinking that everyone else who differed from me was wrong? The situation seemed desperate, for either Christianity with its claim to a special revelation from God was the source and perpetrator of every kind of modern prejudice and bigotry or else there was still some important aspect of Christianity I had failed to understand.

Then to my great relief I came upon a very large but neglected area of traditional Christian understanding which I had never even thought about, but which turned out to hold the key I needed to escape from the dilemma in which I found myself. I came upon the original meaning of an old fashioned concept which, like dogma, has received such a bad press that, along with most everyone else, I had pushed it aside as though it did not exist.

I discovered the exotic concept of heresy and learned that far from being a weapon to condemn those who disagreed with me, it made it possible to appreciate everyone else's beliefs without forcing me to abandon my own. I learned that, contrary to popular opinion, a heresy was not a theological error nor some belief that was wrong, but a belief that was not quite right enough, and that, at least in traditional Christianity, there was no word for wrong belief but only for inadequate belief. Far from being angry with anyone who calls me a heretic, I learned that I ought to run up and embrace him in love and appreciation, for by pointing out that I only understand half the truth at best, he proclaims that the truth is far greater than can be contained in my small mind and that there is still much more for me to learn. I came to see that the very notion of heresy springs from the Christian virtue of hope, for it insists that faith is a continuous journey to be undertaken and not just a present stance to be maintained.

Eventually I came to realize that along with everyone else I have always been a heretic and undoubtedly always will be. I will always be on pilgrimage continually probing the depths of the mystery of God, and I know that others who look into these same depths, no matter what their formal beliefs or religious labels, will see facets of the truth still closed to me. Far from threatening my own faith or discrediting the faith of anyone else, the intellectual humility which comes from recognizing my own heresies makes me face up to my limitations and forces me to appreciate the insights of others.

In practice, however, I find that no matter how much I may wish to appreciate everyone else's beliefs there are some that I simply cannot accept and no amount of broad-minded tolerance is going to make me do so. I dare not go along with those religious beliefs that led a thousand people to drink from a vat of cyanide in Ghana at the end of the Seventies, nor can I respect the beliefs of Satanists practising and encouraging child abuse. And even though I appreciate the views of pacifists, I believe we must do whatever we can to stop people like Hitler and Saddam Hussein massacring and torturing others at will.

I find that no matter how open minded I may wish to be I am constantly judging other people's beliefs. I cannot avoid it, and should I try, I would merely become an accomplice in evil and a friend of falsehood. Instead I have to have some set of standards for judging the ever increasing variety of contradictory and often bizarre beliefs offered in the market place of today's pluralistic society. Unfortunately, however, the standards I adopt are all too often based on little more than my own unfounded and heretical insights. My original broad-minded attempt to appreciate every one else's beliefs all too easily turns in upon itself and becomes the most dangerous heresy of all. By grasping at straws for some standard of judgement I end up nourishing my own most deep seated prejudices.

Here again the concept of heresy has come to my rescue. Just as it helped me appreciate other people's beliefs, so I now found that it also gave me a proper standard for judging these beliefs by again reminding me that falsehood does not come from being totally wrong but from being only partially right. It taught me that there is a wholeness to the truth and a comprehensiveness to reality which every genuine belief must take into account. If my beliefs are really authentic they will encourage me to believe still more and allow me to appreciate the insights enshrined in the beliefs of others.

In judging other people's beliefs I have found that the only thing I need negate are negations and that I must deny nothing except denials. For it is not what any of us actually believes that is wrong but what we deny by our beliefs. I could never, for example, be an extreme Puritan, for though the Puritan is quite right when he insists upon the need for discipline he is terribly wrong when he denies the goodness of earthly pleasures. Nor can I accept the doctrine of re-incarnation, for though it recognizes that human life must go through many forms of existence in order to reach perfection, it denies the eternal value of my own unique personality when it claims that I am forever turning into something other than myself.

In my desire for wholeness I keep coming upon all sorts of popular ideas I cannot accept, no matter how attractive they may appear. I cannot, for example, accept that it is quite alright to get sexually involved with another person without marrying them, for it seems to me that once two people start making love with each other they dare not reject one another later on, and only marriage vows taken seriously are likely to encourage them to think they never will. My very belief in the goodness of sexual love makes we want to ensure that nothing destroys or damages it. In the same sort of way, my belief in the goodness of women and my appreciation of femininity makes it impossible for me to go along with extreme forms of feminism. Because I believe in the goodness of women I do not want to see anyone try to turn them into men.

Contrary to the vague liberal attitude that is currently enjoying a considerable vogue, some attitudes and actions must be roundly condemned, not because they are totally wrong but because they parade themselves as being exclusively right. The trouble with the unrepentant heretic is that he shapes his beliefs to exclude everything he does not fully comprehend and uses his limited knowledge to condemn the insights and understanding of everyone else. In politics he takes the principles of socialism to condemn free enterprise or pursues all the imperatives of free enterprise to further impoverish the poor. In religion he tries to use the bible to destroy the worship of the altar or the altar to ignore the spiritual demands of the bible. In both church and society he uses his inner feelings to rebel against all established authority or else upholds traditional authority to trample down every kind of innovation and renewal.

Heretics become dangerous when they deny that their thinking is heretical. Parading their limited views as the whole truth and their partial insights as the only true orthodoxy, they try to fit everyone else into the strait-jacket of their own blinkered point of view. In so doing they become enemies of the wholeness of the faith and a threat to the peace and unity of mankind. Instead of trying to win others to their own beliefs by rational persuasion these unrepentant heretics devote their energies to knocking down everyone else's beliefs through political confrontation.

Because I crave to grasp hold of all there is to know, and desire to reach out to embrace the entire universe, I cannot accept such exclusiveness. I desire instead what the English call comprehensiveness and others catholicity. I demand wholeness and completeness from life, knowing intuitively that I am made for better things than my own limited experience so far provides, and have the capacity to know what far exceeds the musings of philosophers or the speculations of theologians. I find my vision of the truth more in the writings of poets and my picture of heaven in the works of artists. Yet even here my own poor imagination stretches far beyond the horizons of the Sistine Chapel or the innermost circles of Dante's paradise. I have been given intimations of a future glory greater than anything that can ever be put into words or drawn from the artist's palette.

I said at the beginning that I did not want to argue anyone into Christian belief but only show that it is alright to believe. Now, however, I would like to go a step further and make a plea for wholeness, hoping that you will never be satisfied with your own partial insights and the limitations of your own culture and family background. Examine all your beliefs to see if they open doors into the perception of a reality greater than anything you could have conceived by yourself. Ask yourself if they give you a deeper insight into all the intellectual and spiritual strivings of mankind, an increased appreciation of every man's talent and the achievements of every human civilization.

I have found that Christianity at its best has done exactly this for me. Christ has opened the door to the entire world of personal beliefs and human hopes. As a Christian I can believe what every one else believes and yet believe so much more as well. For I know that all my beliefs are but images of a greater truth, windows into a fuller life. Creeds and sacraments, holy books and formal prayers are but glimpses into eternity. Signs of a glory none of us can now see completely, but which eventually shall end all argument and fulfil every human speculation. "Now", as St Paul tells us, "we see through a glass darkly, but then face to face".

I originally wrote this book for a young man of my parish who now stands before this God of glory. He had little direct experience of the church and used to argue with his friends that in a world where everything can be explained by science there is no reason to believe in God. Then, just after receiving a scholarship to Oxford University, he developed a malignant brain tumour which the surgeons could not completely remove and which no other kind of cancer therapy was able to touch. Before his death I regularly gave him laying-on-of-hands for healing, and after about the third time he said to me, "You know, I think I am beginning to believe in all this. I am so much better after each time I am blessed."

It turned out that Nick Greenwood did not need to read this book. God's healing power became for him an inward spiritual reality which needed no defence from reasoned argument. As the cancer took over more and more, so day by day he became more content within himself and more at peace with God, his family and his friends. For those of us who looked on from the outside it began to seem as though he was losing all sense of the past and indeed all sense of time. But in talking to him it became obvious that Nick was simply living closer to eternity where there is neither past nor future but only the present moment. And in those moments he talked about his friends being with him and the parties he was going to.

Then one night it sounded as though he was carrying on a long conversation with some unknown people, and when his father asked who they were he simply said that he was talking to some new friends who had told him they were waiting for him. Two days later, when his body could no longer sustain him, he entered into the wholeness of eternity where all his imaginings became real for the first time and all his dreams came true.

Belief in some sort of God comes from reasoned argument, but faith begins with dreams and ends in eternity. For now all we dare ask is that our dreams are vindicated by the undoubted action of God in our lives and in the lives of those around us. In exchange, all that God asks of us is that no matter what may befall us we continue reaching out to "taste and see that the Lord is good".

BELIEVE IT OR NOT

The Light of Christ

11

A New Beginning

This might seem to be the end of the story but in reality it is only the beginning. All I have tried to do until now is show that it is alright to believe. The next step is to find out whether or not Christian beliefs really are right, and no amount of argument or demonstration can decide that. All you can do is walk the road of faith yourself and see where it leads.

Your journey will begin with many questions still left unanswered, but I do not believe that this should trouble you or make you hesitate. The way forward in our understanding of God does not lie in having all our questions answered before we begin the journey, but by continuing to ask questions as long as the journey lasts.

I have found the journey of faith to be rather like those computer games in which, after every move, the player has to find the answer to a new problem or decide which way to move next. The answer to each question takes him a step further along his way, but with every step a new question arises. So it goes to the end of the game when at last he finds the hidden treasure or goes into the royal castle or enters the kingdom of heaven. The questions and answers are part of the game itself and if he refuses to play until all his questions are answered he will never find his reward.

I know of several people who have never started the journey of faith because they have insisted that before they begin, every question must be answered and every argument proven. Rather like stubborn children, they refuse to walk until they are able to run and will not set out on the journey until they are certain of their reward at the end. Too timid to take any risks, they keep wandering about in circles getting nowhere, demanding answers to every question that comes into their heads before they dare move towards anything of real value or importance.

Real flesh and blood children, of course, never act like this. They walk before they begin to run, and learn to walk by taking one step at a time. All of us started out on our spiritual lives like this as well, asking one question at a time. But then, when answers were slow in coming, many of us gave up asking any more questions and settled down at some wayside inn, the journey of faith unfinished and our inner desires unsatisfied. Now if we are to take up the journey once more, we must go back to our childhood and learn to ask all the important questions once again, pausing at every stage in our travels to understand what we have discovered, but never insisting that all our questions are answered at once.

If then you think that the Christian faith might just make some kind of sense, your next step is to risk testing this faith by your own individual experience. For though Christianity is grounded in reason only experience can ever convince us that it is true. Yet our own experience is far too limited by our personal circumstances and individual temperament ever to be the final test of anything. Rather than attempt to travel the road of faith by ourselves we must enter into the experience of all those others who have travelled along that same road before us. Faith's journey must take place within the Christian community, for only among those who already believe, can we see how faith actually works in practice.

A New Beginning

Symbolically the journey begins with a baptism of water and the spirit, which ever since New Testament times Christians have always described as a kind of second birth. Originally the baptismal ceremonies and the experience of rebirth were so closely tied together that one was clearly a sign of the other. By baptism a person became a member of a new community with its own unique cultural and social identity. He entered into a new set of personal relationships often more intense than those of his own natural family, and was given a new name, his "Christian name", which represented a new character and a new personality. In the very deepest sense he was "born again".

In the first centuries of the church's life, when being a Christian was treated as an act of treason punishable by death, it was not easy to become a member of this new outlawed community. Your initial interest might be aroused when you began to notice a strange difference in one of your closest friends, or perhaps in your own slave, which you found difficult to describe but irresistibly intriguing and attractive. Upon pressing your friend or slave to explain this change he finally admits that he has become a Christian and eventually you decide to look into this new secret society yourself. You are told something of the risks involved and the discipline required, but you still persist. Finally they take you to one of their secret gatherings in a large house on the other side of town. Here to your surprise you find several of your own personal acquaintances, including both your neighbour's two slaves and several important town officials. The local plumber, who turns out to be the leader of the group and is called the overseer or bishop, quizzes you about your intentions, and then, finally convinced of your sincerity and integrity, he allows you to come to weekly meetings for instruction.

These meetings, in which, beginning with the book of Genesis, all the scriptures are explained, are likely to last two or three years. During this time, after several of your fellow students have been captured by the police and summarily executed, you are made dramatically aware of the risk you yourself will be taking by becoming a Christian. Still you persist, and eventually the time comes when you are asked if you genuinely desire to become a member of the Christian church. You say that you do, the members of the local community vote to accept you as someone they can trust, and the day of your baptism draws near.

On a Saturday afternoon you go to the bishop's house and renounce all the ways in which you are still tied to your past life. You renounce forever the gods of this world, the idolatry of your own appetites, and all the works of the devil. Exorcisms are said over you to drive away any evil spirits, and then you are told that you must not eat or drink anything until after you are baptised early the next morning. It is as though you must rid yourself of even the natural food which has sustained your previous life, for this is to be a new beginning and a new birth, and nothing of the old must remain.

That evening, still having no idea what is going to happen, you gather with your fellow candidates and spend the night together in final instruction and prayer. Then, very early in the morning whilst it is still dark, you are led into another part of the house where there is a large pool of water. There you are stripped of all your clothes and made completely vulnerable, with no protective clothing and nothing you can hide from others. Nothing is left of your old life.

Healing and protective oil is then poured over you as it was over the ancient athletes, and, as the first rays of dawn come through the windows, you are taken by the hand down into the pool where you are immersed in water in the name of the Father who made you and all the world, of the Son who redeemed you and all mankind, and of the Holy Spirit who will make you holy along with all the faithful. You rise up from the other side of the pool and a white garment is placed over you, symbolising a new life and membership in a new community. You are given a lighted candle representing Christ as the light of the world, and then, as a new born member of the Christian family, you are fed with a spoonful of milk and honey, the baby formula of the day, for though you may be old in years, you have again become a little child starting off on the road of faith.

Holding your own lighted candle, you and the other candidates are taken into the main hall of the house where all the members of the community are assembled. Amidst a sea of lighted candles you move to the front of the room where the bishop is seated before an altar. He lays his hands upon your head and gives you the spirit of the community or, as the French call it, the community's "esprit de corps" which is none other than the Holy Spirit which God the Father sent into the church at the very beginning and which continues to make it the resurrected body of Christ Himself. Having received this Holy Spirit of the Christian community, you next exchange the peace of Christ with your fellow Christians and together with them offer bread and wine upon the altar. Then, for the first time in your life, you witness and take part in the performance of those secret rites known as the Christian Mysteries, for which Christians are persecuted daily and in defence of which many of your closest friends have died. Yet these rites turn out to be so very simple. The bishop blesses bread and wine, saying over them the words by which Jesus proclaimed that they were his body and blood, and then you are fed with "The Body of Christ, the bread of heaven" and you drink "The Blood of Christ, the cup of salvation".

That is all there is to it, but by the time it is finished a new day has dawned and a new life begun. You know in your heart of hearts that what has been celebrated today is not just the day of Christ's resurrection but your own resurrection as well. In the waters of baptism you have been buried with him, and from these waters you have risen to new life. To live that new life a new Spirit has been poured into you which is God the Holy Spirit who gives life to all the People of God. You have become a member of a new super-race originating in another world which Jesus called the Kingdom of Heaven. In that kingdom you are sustained by other worldly food and drink which is none other than the actual Body and Blood of your God. This Day of Resurrection is only a beginning. In the days and years to come you will continue on your journey of faith, but now you will be walking in the Spirit of a new family and of a new nation. As St Peter once told those who had just been baptised, "You are a royal nation, a holy priesthood, an amazing people".

Just as we are united with one another by a school spirit or team spirit, so these early Christians were united by a special spirit governing the life of this new community into which they had been baptized, and their experience of its common life forced them to believe that this spirit was none other than God Himself, the Holy Spirit. In baptism the old spirit of the world, which previously governed everything they did, had now been killed forever and the Holy Spirit had begun to take over their lives. For them the quality of their new life in the Spirit was the final evidence for faith and the only certain proof that the God discovered by the ancient Jews really is the one true God.

After Jesus' resurrection those who were initiated into the church were forced to conclude that the Holy Spirit who animated this new body of Christ was the same God who had been working in Jesus from the beginning. And just as Jesus had played a part in the life of our humanity from the moment of his conception so this same Holy Spirit, ruling the lives of his followers since the moment of their baptism, gave them a part to play in the divine life of God Himself. By offering their bread and wine, the result of all their labours, on the altar of Christian sacrifice, they themselves actually became the Body and Blood of their God through the transforming power of this same Holy Spirit. What Adam and Eve had been unable to do by themselves, these early Christians discovered had been done for them. Through their life in the church they had become as gods and that human desire to be divine, instead of ending in sin and death, now led to new life in the power of the resurrected Christ.

Through the Holy Spirit they had a new energy and a new strength. He led them into all truth so that now they saw everything from the new perspective of hope. They were able to do the works of sacrificial love that Jesus himself had done, and, as he had promised, they were able to do even greater works than these. As members of Jesus' new resurrected body on earth they were no longer limited, as Jesus had been, by the confines of an individual neighbourhood in a particular country at a single moment of time. By the power of the Holy Spirit the new Christian community swiftly spread throughout the whole world, accomplishing in all places throughout the ages the wonderful works of God.

So at least it seemed to those early Christians who found themselves gradually transformed by a power they could not explain. They knew that the change within them could not have come through their own efforts, for that way usually led to disaster. Nor was it through the charisma of their church's leaders who, on the whole, were anything but charismatic, and it certainly was not created by some organised psychological gimmick because they did not have any in those days. It seemed obvious to them, that this personal transformation could only have come about through the Holy Spirit they had received at their baptism when they were adopted into a new order of peace and love, a supernatural order created by the same Spirit on the Day of Pentecost when Mary and the apostles were gathered together in the upper room.

The personal experience of the transforming power of the Holy Spirit convinced these early Christians that Jesus was alive and working among them. But is it possible for us to have this same experience today? By now that Spirit which was given to the Christian church 2,000 years ago is so intermingled with the spirit of our everyday secular world that there seems no easy way to distinguish one from the other. Because we can no longer plunge someone into a new way of life through some dramatic rite of initiation, it never occurs to most people, at least in England, that in baptism they might become members of some special kind of spirit-filled community. Even those who consider themselves to be "church-goers" rarely think of themselves as actual members of a special community, any more than going to the cinema makes them members of a theatre community. At best they might decide to become friends or even patrons of either, but it would never occur to them to think of themselves as actual members. In a church where ordination rather than baptism has become the new initiation rite and only the clergy are said to "enter the church", membership is left to the professionals. For the rest of the population baptismal initiation has been replaced by "having the baby done", and talk about "lay ministry" usually does little more than treat the more committed members of the church as though they were ordained clergy without pay.

It is possible, of course, to restore all the outward ceremonies of the original rite of initiation at Easter Vigil services when, during the middle of the night, adults and children are baptised, confirmed and receive their first holy communion, and this can be a very moving occasion, in which the candidate gains a wonderful sense of receiving a Spirit not of this world, and of being lifted into the very presence of God. Yet, when the service of initiation is over, life in the church carries on exactly as before. There are no new mysteries that the candidate has not already experienced and, except for receiving communion, nothing in his life has really changed.

Because Christian initiation these days rarely gives people any lasting experience of the power of the Holy Spirit, many Christians have started talking about a separate "Baptism of the Spirit", and some actually claim that only those who have received this baptism are real Christians and true members of the church. Usually, they themselves have had some kind of powerful conversion experience, which has suddenly redirected their whole lives towards God, convincing them that even though they may not yet be very good Christians, their lives are empowered by a Spirit not of this world. An inner experience of the living God gives them a certainty which cannot be shaken by any kind of rational argument or personal disaster. Knowing already the active power of God in their lives, they do not need to read a book such as this, nor are they inclined to think that anyone else need read it either. God, they believe, will not be known by any kind of evidence I or anyone else can offer, but only through a personal conversion similar to their own.

For those who believe they have been baptised in the Holy Spirit, and there are many thousands of them, this experience is sufficient reason for entrusting their whole life to Jesus. It is of no help however, to those of us who have never had such an experience, and yet who are desperately looking for some kind of purpose in our lives; we who are constantly searching for the fulfilment of our desires and dreams. Nor does it answer the doubts of those who once believed they had such an experience but, either through the weight of everyday responsibilities and disappointments, or through the arguments of friends, or perhaps disillusionment with their fellow Christians, have gradually lost their original certainty of faith and become indifferent towards God and their fellow Christians. It is no good claiming that these people have given way to the devil, as is sometimes said. More often than not they fervently wish their original confidence could be restored, but are unable to find any way in which this can possibly happen. With nostalgia they look back to former happier times when for a moment it seemed as though God really was in his heaven and all was right with the world.

I believe that the heart of Jesus goes out to all these people just as fervently as it does to the fully committed. Perhaps even more so, for if Jesus is God the Creator then surely he loves all the people he has made, and gives himself to everyone with no conditions laid down and no strings attached. His Holy Spirit must be available to everyone, so that we can all have that certainty of faith which, for reason operating by itself, must forever remain only a possibility.

If you are one of those people who think it is just possible that the Christian Faith may be true, but still cannot find any way of being certain that it is, then I hope you will not be afraid to take these first steps on the pilgrimage of faith, to test the spirits of the committed, whether or not they are of God. Become involved in the life of the Christian community; find out if over and above the spirit of dissension, bitterness and pettiness which you find, there is also a spirit greater than these, a Holy Spirit which, at the end of the day, overcomes all opposition and all discouragement. Begin to talk to God as though he is the reality He is claimed to be, and instead of depending upon the uninformed hearsay of others, take advantage of every opportunity to learn more about what the Christian faith is really all about.

Then, when you have taken this first step, do not become discouraged if nothing changes in your life all at once. For some people God's action apparently hits them like a bolt of lightning, but for most of us there is only a slow gradual process of recognition. Persevere in your search for faith, but always with the hope that the time will come when you can commit yourself totally to the God of the ancient Jews, fully revealed in the living Christ by the Holy Spirit working within you.

For Further Reading

What follows is neither a comprehensive bibliography nor even a list of titles I have used in writing this book. Here, rather, are a few works I have found especially helpful in my own pilgrimage of faith and which I believe have stood, or are likely to stand, the test of time.

On Christian Belief:

G.K. Chesterton,
...*Orthodoxy* (John Lane, London 1909)
C.S. Lewis,
...*Mere Christianity* (Geoffrey Bles, London 1952)
John Macquarrie,
...*The Faith of the People of God*
(SCM Press, London 1972)
...*Principles of Christian Theology*
(SCM Press, London 1966)

On Pilgrimage

J.R.R. Tolkien,
...*The Lord of the Rings*
(George Allen & Unwin Ltd, London 1954)

ON REASON AND EXPERIENCE:

>Harry Blamires,
>...*The Christian Mind* (SPCK, London 1963)
>F. Dostoevsky,
>...'Notes from Underground' in *The Short Novels of Dostoevsky* (Dial Press, N.Y. 1951)
>R.D. Laing,
>...*The Politics of Experience and the Bird of Paradise*
>(Penguin Books, Harmondsworth 1967)
>John Macmurray,
>...*The Self as Agent* (Faber and Faber, London 1957)
>...*Persons in Relation*
>(Faber and Faber, London 1961)

ON THE MEANING OF DOGMA:

>V.A. Demant,
>...Introduction to *The Religious Prospect*
>(Frederick Muller Ltd, London 1939)
>T.E. Hulme,
>...'Humanism and the Religious Attitude' in *Speculations,* ed. Herbert Read
>(Routledge and Kegan Paul, London 1924)

ON GOD AS REALITY

>Bede Frost,
>...*Who? A Book about God*
>(A.R. Mowbray & Co, London & Oxford 1940)
>Etienne Gilson,
>...*The Spirit of Medieaval Philosophy,* trans. A.H.C. Downes (Sheed & Ward, London 1936)

ON GOD AS REALITY (CONTINUED)

E.L. Mascall,
...*He Who Is*
(Longmans, Green and Co., London 1943)
Dorothy L. Sayers,
...*The Mind of the Maker*
(Methuen & Co., London 1941)

ON THE NATURE OF RELIGION:

Mircea Eliade,
...*The Sacred and the Profane,* trans. William R. Trask (Harcourt, Brace and Company, N.Y. 1959)
Rudolph Otto,
...*The Idea of the Holy,* trans. J.W. Harvey
(Oxford University Press, London 1923)
Wilfred Cantwell Smith,
...*The Meaning and End of Religion*
(Macmillian Company, N.Y. 1962)
Joachim Wach,
...*Sociology of Religion*
(The University of Chicago Press, Chicago Illinois 1944)

ON THE DESTRUCTION OF OUR HUMANITY:

T.S. Eliot,
...'The Wasteland' in *The Collected Poems 1909 - 1935* (Faber and Faber, London 1936)
C.S. Lewis,
...*The Abolition of Man* [New Edt.]
(Geoffrey Bles, London 1946)

ON THE JEWISH UNDERSTANDING OF GOD:

> Gerrard von Rad,
> ...*Old Testament Theology*, trans. D.M.G. Stalker
> (Oliver & Boyd, Edinburgh & London 2 vols.,
> 1962, 65)

ON THE NATURE OF REVELATION:

> Louis Bouyer,
> ...*The Meaning of Sacred Scripture,* trans. Mary Perkins
> (University of Notre Dame Press, Notre Dame, Indiana 1958)
> E. Schillebeeckx,
> ...*Revelation and Theology,* Vol.1, Pt.1
> (Sheed & Ward, London and New York 1967)

ON THE NATURE OF FAITH:

> Austin Farrer,
> ...*Glass of Vision* (Dacre Press, London 1948)
> ...*Faith and Speculation* (A & C Black, London 1967)
> John Hick,
> ...*Faith and Knowledge* 2nd edition
> (Macmillan Press, London 1988)
> Scott Holland,
> ...'Faith' in *Lux Mundi. A Series of Studies on the Religion of the Incarnation,* ed. Charles Gore
> (John Murray, London 1889)

SUGGESTIONS FOR FURTHER READING

ON THE PROBLEM OF EVIL:

>F. Dostoevsky,
>...*Brothers Karamazov*, trans. Constance Garnett
>(J.M. Dent & Sons, London 1927)
>Austin Farrer,
>...*Love Almighty & Ills Unlimited*
>(Doubleday & Co., Garden City, New York 1961;
>Collins London 1962)

ON THE PROBLEM OF PAIN:

>C.S. Lewis,
>...*The Problem of Pain* (Centenary Press, London 1940)
>C.S. Lewis
>...*A Grief Observed* (Faber and Faber, London 1961)

ON THE MEANING OF LOVE

>Hans Urs von Balthasar,
>...*Love Alone: The Way of Revelation. A Theological Perspective*, ed. Alexander Dru
>(Burns & Oates, London 1968)
>C.S. Lewis,
>...*The Four Loves* (Geoffrey Bless, London 1960)
>Rollo May,
>...*Love and Will* (W.W. Norton & Company, N. Y. 1969)

ON SACRIFICE:

>F.C.N. Hicks,
>...*The Fullness of Sacrifice* (SPCK, London 1959)
>E.O James,
>...*Sacrifice and Sacrament*
>(Thames and Hudson, London 1962)

ON THE INCARNATION

> J. Austin Baker,
> ...*The Foolishness of God* (Collins, London 1970)
> Charles Williams,
> ...*He Came Down from Heaven, and The Forgiveness of Sins* (Faber & Faber, London 1950)
> ...*St Athanasius on the Incarnation*, trans. and ed. by A Religious of the C.S.M.V. (Geoffrey Bless, London 1944)

ON THE LIFE OF CHRIST:

> Dorothy L. Sayers,
> ...*The Man Born to be King. A Play-cycle on the Life of our Lord and Saviour Jesus Christ* (Victor Gollancz, London 1943)

ON CHRIST AND THE EVOLUTION OF MAN:

> Teilhard de Chardin,
> ...*The Phenomenon of Man*
> (Wm. Collins Sons & Co., London 1959)
> Austin Farrer,
> ...*A Science of God?* (Geoffrey Bless, London 1966)

ON THE RESURRECTION:

> Frank Morison,
> ...*Who Moved the Stone?*
> (Faber and Faber, London 1930)
> Rowan Williams,
> ...*Resurrection*
> (Darton, Longman and Todd, London 1982)

SUGGESTIONS FOR FURTHER READING

ON MAN'S SUPERNATURAL DESTINY:

Teilhard de Chardin,
...*The Divine Milieu*
(Wm. Collins Sons & Co., London 1960)
C.S. Lewis,
...*The Great Divorce* (Geoffrey Bless, London 1945)
E.L. Mascall,
...*Nature and Supernature*
(Darton, Longman & Todd, London 1976)

ON CHRIST AND THE CHURCH:

G.K. Chesterton,
...*The Everlasting Man*, Pt2,
(Hodder and Stoughton, London 1925)
T.S. Eliot,
...'Choruses from The Rock' *op. cit.*
E. Schillebeeckx,
...*Christ the Sacrament of Encounter with God*, trans.
Paul Barrett & N.D. Smith
(Sheed and Ward, London & New York 1963)

ON CHRISTIANITY AND OTHER RELIGIONS:

G.K. Chesterton,
...'The Ballad of the White Horse' in *The Collected Poems of G.K.Chesterton*
(Cecil Palmer, London 1927)
...*The Everlasting Man,* Pt 1. *Op. Cit.*
E.O. James,
...*Christianity and other Religions*
(Hodder and Stoughton, London 1968)

ON THE CATHOLICITY OF CHRISTIANITY:

    A.G. Hebert,
    ...*The Form of the Church,*
    (Faber and Faber, London 1944)
    A. M. Ramsey,
    ...*The Gospel and the Catholic Church*
    (Longmans, Green and Co., London 1936)

ON THE HOLY SPIRIT IN THE CHURCH:
    A. M. Ramsey,
    ...*Holy Spirit* (SPCK, London 1977)